THE CALL OF A Woman

Published by Buffalo River Publishing

Paperback ISBN: 978-1-7394426-0-6
ePub ISBN: 978-1-7394426-1-3

British Library Cataloguing-in-Publication data
A catalogue record for this book is available from the British Library.

Acknowledgments - see page 166

Cover design and typeset by Spiffing Covers

Cover photographer: Felipe Cespedes sourced at www.pexels.com

THE CALL OF A *Woman*

Walking in Your God-Given Identity and Calling

RENAY TAYLOR

To every woman who's known that there's much more in her that needs to be expressed and lived,
To all the mothers and grandmothers through whom nations were birthed and histories changed,
To every woman throughout the generations who has labored and run the race,
To my strong and beautiful sisters Melaney, Leandre, Taryn and Karlene,
To my mother whose intuition and fortitude has taught me much,

This book is dedicated to you.

Contents

Before we begin......

Thank you for setting time apart to explore more about your identity as a woman of God and the calling he has called you to.

This book was born out of my own questions - and the enquiries of countless women I have talked with, taught, coached, mentored and prayed with over the years - about our role as Christian women in God's kingdom purposes. I have written this book within my present understanding of what the entirety of the scriptures reveal about God's mandate for us as women, his daughters and female image bearers. I too, as we all are, continue in this journey of unlearning and re-learning, prayerfully seeking insight and discernment about the calling that God has given us.

This book is written with the acknowledgement that tensions exist between select translated biblical scriptures, and that this tension is something that continues to challenge the church in its desire to serve God as faithfully as it can. This book aims to encourage a continued active exploration of women's calling and mandate and their role in the advancement of God's kingdom.

Jesus used simple parables based on everyday life scenarios to communicate biblical truths. This practical book is written in a simple, straightforward style with the aim of making it very readable and accessible to you, the reader. Wherever biblical scripture is included in the text, the NIV translation is referenced, unless otherwise indicated.

An application workbook is included at the back of this book to support further reflection about the contents of each chapter and what this means for you and your life. And to further assist you as you start to explore your unique calling in God, an additional worksheet for this is also included.

May the thoughts and ideas contained in this book encourage you and affirm your value and your place in God's kingdom purpose. The world needs you and all that God has placed in you and mandated you to do.

Be blessed.

Renay

PART 1

Women's God-Given Identity and Calling

Introduction

The race

Your palms are sweaty. Your heart is racing. Your face is set like flint. There's a breeze blowing through your hair. You feel determined. You feel nervous. You feel excited. You don't know what the race will be like, what your fellow runners will be like, what the final outcome will be. But you are determined to give it your all, to persevere no matter what. You are going to run to win!

The clack of the gun goes, and you're off! You push off the starting blocks and let your legs find their rhythm, straining, pushing. This is the race of your life. Everything you have experienced thus far, everything you've trained for, has brought you to this moment.

You were always running, running, running. Since you were a little kid. Always challenging adults and peers alike to a race. You were fast. You ran to win. Your parents encouraged your talent and interests by enrolling you in the local athletics club.

Your coaches taught you all you know about understanding your potential, good technique and honing your particular running style.

You put in the practise. It was hard work, but you enjoyed it. It was something you loved to do. It brought you joy. You were gifted at it.

You were successful. Others recognised your gift. They recognised your hard work. They encouraged you. They prayed over you. You won medals in the amateur, local and regional track and field events.

And now here you are, going for the big league. Your first professional race. And you're ready to grow, stretch, win!

This is the race of your life. Everything you have experienced and practised for, has brought you to this moment. And you're running with all the power within you. You're running full out. You know the power in you and you're ready to let it all come out on that track.

But no sooner have you left the starting blocks and the race becomes confusing. At the 100m mark a race marshal flags you and motions that you need to stay in your lane, you can only run in the outer lanes. Then at the halfway mark in the race another marshal stops you and says that you can run up to here and no further. Your skill and gifting are good enough to enter this race, but you can only go up to here in the race. You can run full out on the spot if you like, but you can't run further, you can't run towards the finish line. You can't get the chance to test how far you can ultimately go with your gift, talent and passion for running.

You look around, confused, at the other female athletes bundled together with you at that spot on the track. All as bewildered as you are. Some women stand there with a resigned lowered head, avoiding eye contact, avoiding any conversation about this strange situation you all find yourselves in. Afraid that any conversation about this may result in their complete disqualification and banning from future races.

Your confusion increases as you see the male athletes in the inner lane, running full out towards the finish line, faces set as flint, straining with every inch of skill, power and will within them to finish the race, to win the prize. And you recognise among the group of male athletes peers you had out run in the heats. Whose stride and natural power were no match to yours. Who had to put in so much extra effort in training. Whom you had mentored and supported. And they get to run full out. They get to finish in the professional leagues, the national leagues, the international leagues.

While you are relegated to the amateur and regional leagues, running in designated lanes only, with a limited race distance.

And you're left there standing, wondering why.

The Christian walk is often like this for many women. We believe the apostle Paul's words when he says that we too, like him, are to run with perseverance the race marked out for us as Christians. Running to win, straining towards the prize to which God has called us. Fixing our eyes on Jesus, the pioneer and perfecter of our faith[1].

But then in bewilderment, as we walk in the calling we believe we have received, our experience is many times one of a relegation to the side lines, and the diminishing of our voice, gifting, talents and calling.

And we are left wondering, 'Whose race we are actually running?'[2]

Calling

As daughters of God we know we are called by him, unto him and unto the people of this world, for his glory and for his kingdom. In Romans 14: 8 we read, '*For if we live, we live to the Lord, and if we die, we die to the Lord. So then, whether we live or whether we die, we are the Lord's*'.

In walking in our calling we find our purpose during this earthly life. But what exactly is our calling?

The Merriam-Webster dictionary[3] defines calling as, '*a strong inner impulse toward a particular course of action especially when accompanied by conviction of divine influence*'.

Ephesians 2:10 (NLT) tells us, '*For we are God's masterpiece. He has created us anew in Christ Jesus, so we can do the good things he planned for us long ago*'.

We are created by God and also redeemed by God[4]. We are his masterpiece. God designed each one of us for a life of purpose and significance.

As Christians we have two types of calling – a *General* calling and a *Unique*, *Specific* calling.

First, there is our **General Calling[5].** This is our *primary* calling unto God and unto others as disciples of God. God chose us and loved us first, even before the foundations of the earth. We are called unto God as sons and daughters and find our salvation in him. As sons and daughters who have been born again spiritually in Jesus, we are called to love God with all our heart, soul, mind and strength[6] – that is, in our wholehearted love of God and as disciples of Christ we fully submit our lives and will to him.

As Jesus' disciples we are also called to love others as God loves us, and to share the good news and make disciples wherever we may find ourselves[7]. This is an act of love and service for the benefit and upliftment of others, and in recognition that just like us they were created by God in his image and are loved by him. This calling unites all believers, the Body of Christ, in a common mission on earth under the lordship of our Savior.

In Matthew 16: 16-19 (NKJV)[8], when Jesus declared the mission for his believers, he used the Greek word *ekklesia* (ἐκκλησία, ας, ἡ)[9] - commonly written in English texts as **ecclesia** - to refer to the future global body of believers he was building: '*...on this rock I will build my church (ecclesia), and the gates of Hades shall not prevail against it*'. This word ecclesia means '*the ones who are called out*', and at the time of Jesus it referred to the political assembly of citizens of a secular Greek state operating in the marketplace in a governmental capacity. Thus the ecclesia, translated as *church* in the English biblical text, does not refer to a building, institution or organisation with services and offices which we understand as the contemporary corporate church. Rather, it profoundly refers to a global body of called out, set apart believers in Christ who act as God's righteous governance in the world, operating in the power of the Spirit[10]. (For clarity, throughout this book where the term *church* is used it refers to the contemporary corporate church organisation as opposed to the ecclesia).

This ecclesia's calling is deeply rooted in our identity in God[11] - who we are in him, and the authority and responsibility we have to demonstrate God's image on earth, and to bring his kingdom to all, including the disadvantaged, the marginalised and the disempowered. A holy people living intentionally, proactively and strategically engaging with the marketplace. Jesus chose this ecclesia to be his redemptive, restorative agency by which the world would be transformed, and the kingdom of God would be realised. Where even two or three believers gather[12] in such unity of purpose in the marketplace, there God is manifest powerfully.

It is within the context of that general calling as the ecclesia of believers, that we find **our Unique, Specific Calling** as individuals. In this calling, God uniquely equips each one of us to work out our general calling in the most effective way, using our particular spiritual gifts, passions, strengths and talents within the specific spheres of influence and impact he grants us. Whether that be in our homes, serving in the corporate church, or serving in the marketplace and various sectors of society he qualifies and equips us for. It is done so that unreached souls and societal needs can be met, and human society develops and is transformed in God's righteous agenda.

Where our specific calling is in the marketplace, this may be worked out within the sphere of influence we have within a chosen vocation, profession or trade we occupy within a season of life. A specific calling can drastically change the course of your life, and the journey may not be straightforward. As with all things, our calling is never static or fixed, but it may shift or change through various seasons[13] throughout our lifetime. Discerning and navigating our specific calling can feel challenging at times, which is why this is often a topic of much discussion, prayer and soul searching.

It is complicated enough working out and prayerfully discerning your calling in Christ in a particular life season, without the added seemingly arbitrary restrictions, prohibitions and limitations that we discover may be placed on us as women. Especially where these may seem to be in conflict with what we believe God is calling us to - what we believe God has been stirring in us, what we believe we are gifted for, what we are passionate about, what we excel at, where we feel there is a societal need, and where we have seen proof of positive impact and God's anointing on our efforts.

This can be confusing, as we try to run the race set before us as daughters of Christ. And we are caused to wonder,

What are we called to as women of God?

What is our mandate in God's kingdom purposes?

What is our role in his ecclesia?

And amid this confusion, God asks you today, '*Who knit you together in your mother's womb? Who called you? Who knows you by name?*'[14]

Here's the thing: God knew who you were and what you're made for long before the world told you who you are[15]. Before the voices of your parents, family members, teachers, peers, friends, colleagues and even the church told you who you may be.

Woman of God, the only truth that matters about who you are is what God says and demonstrates in the scriptures about who you are in him. To step into our purpose and walk in our calling we first need to understand our identity in God. If we do not understand and embrace our identity as sons and daughters of God, made in his image, we'll be persuaded to make sense of who we are, and what we are called to, outside of this divine design and purpose.

This book is the start of that journey of exploration for you, my fellow sister in Christ.

St Augustine declared that '*the Old Testament is revealed in the New Testament, and the New Testament is veiled in the Old Testament*'. God is the same yesterday, today and forever[16] and his promises are yes and amen to those that believe. Thus, to understand what God says and demonstrates about the identity and calling we have as women, we need to take a perspective from across the entirety of the scriptures. In the chapters of this book we are going to examine what the bible tells us about the call on women and the role we play in God's kingdom, by exploring what we can learn about,

- God's intended purposes when he created us in the Garden of Eden,
- The ministry of women recorded in the Old Testament,
- Jesus' approach to women during his earthly ministry,
- The role women played in the 1st century New Testament church, and
- What the scriptures tell us about our role in the latter days (the times we are in today).

We'll also examine more closely the lived calling of one woman in the bible to explore the lessons we can glean for ourselves as we endeavour to live out our own calling as women.

So let's dive in.

CHAPTER 1

In the Beginning

It happened on the sixth day
The everlasting God created two human beings
In his own image
Male and Female
With a mandate from him
To inhabit this earth
To have dominion over it
To be fruitful and multiply
To reflect his glory.

It happened on the sixth day
The God of all creation said, 'It is not good'
It is *not good* for my male image bearer to be alone
It is *not good* that there's no suitable helper for him
It is *not good* for a man to be alone in the mandate
It is *not good.*

It happened on the sixth day
That a suitable helper was created
A woman
Fearfully and wonderfully made
In God's own image
God's suitable female image bearer
And the man was no longer alone in the mandate
And creation was complete
And the God of all creation said, 'It is *very good*'.

It happened on the sixth day.

Divine design

The Genesis 1-2 account of God's divine design is amazing. Amazing in what it reveals of God's nature, his creation intent and the mandate for us as women (and men).

In Genesis 1: 26-28 we read,

> '*Then God said, "Let us make mankind in our image, in our likeness, so that they may rule over the fish in the sea and the birds in the sky, over the livestock and all the wild animals, and over all the creatures that move along the ground."*
>
> *So God created mankind in his own image, in the image of God he created them; male and female he created them.*
>
> *God blessed them and said to them, "Be fruitful and increase in number; fill the earth and subdue it. Rule over the fish in the sea and the birds in the sky and over every living creature that moves on the ground."*'

Similarly, Genesis 5: 1-2 summarises this as such,

> '*When God created mankind, he made them in the likeness of God. He created them male and female and blessed them. And he named them "Mankind" when they were created.*'

Three things are revealed and declared in these passages:

- The nature and image of God – holy trinity, male and female
- We are all made in this image of God – male and female
- We have all been given the dominion mandate over the earth

The image and likeness of God

The first biblical recording of the creation of human beings in Genesis 1: 26-28 is framed here together with the first revelation of two aspects of the nature of God.

Firstly, it contains the first biblical reference to the triune nature of God - the Holy Trinity of the Father, Son and Holy Spirit. 'Let *us* make man in *our* image, in *our* likeness……' Plural. Three in one. Existing and operating in harmony and unity as one. None higher than the other. There exists no hierarchy or superiority in the Trinity.

Secondly, we learn that God's nature is both male and female[1]. 'So God created man (mankind) *in his own image ……… male and female* he created *them*'. Like two sides of the same coin. Two distinct aspects of the one same essence. There is no indication here either of any superiority of one of these aspects of God over the other, or that either gender held a greater proportion of God's nature or qualities than the other.

Made in God's image and likeness

I believe it is significant, and no small coincidence, that when the Bible records that the divine design was that men and women were made in God's image and likeness, that very same passage simultaneously also reveals for the first time what that image and likeness entails.

God is leaving us clues as to what his intention is for the creation and design of men and women. We are God's divine design. Male and Female. Made in God's image and likeness – a triune God in whom there is no hierarchy and superiority among the three persons of the Trinity.

We are made to exist as God's image bearers. If we are truly made in the image of God, then each man and woman is created with inherent dignity, value and worth. How we understand our origin has a fundamental influence on how we should live. God's design for us was to operate in unity and harmony, as he operates in unity and harmony, with no hierarchy between the image bearers of God. The destinies of men and women are inextricably linked, and the full understanding of women's Godly identity and who women truly are is crucial to the destinies of both men and women. Both are equally required and needed to reflect God fully.

The dominion mandate

The dominion mandate in Genesis 1: 26-30 was given to both the male and female God created[2].

> '*God blessed them and said to them, "Be fruitful and increase in number; fill the earth and subdue it. Rule over the fish in the sea and the birds in the sky and over every living creature that moves on the ground."*
>
> *Then God said, "I give you every seed-bearing plant on the face of the whole earth and every tree that has fruit with seed in it. They will be yours for food. And to all the beasts of the earth and all the birds in the sky and all the creatures that move along the ground—everything that has the breath of life in it—I give every green plant for food." And it was so*'.

Yes, it *was* so. God gave *them* a mandate, both the man and the woman he created - to be fruitful, to multiply, to *rule* over every living creature and to *subdue* the earth. To rule and subdue. In other words, to have control, dominion, rulership and leadership over the earth, including dominion over principalities and powers on the earth. Both were given the mandate, the authority to carry out God's commission, and to rule and have control over the earth. Both of them. There's no hierarchy or superiority in this commission expressed in this passage.

It is incredible even today how many churches are still teaching that only Adam was given the dominion mandate. And it amazes me each time I take a group on a read-through of these Genesis passages, how many surprised faces and lightbulb moments I see – so many women have no idea that the Bible clearly states that 'God said to *them*'.

Which Bible are we reading and being taught from? And why oh why would anyone teaching this passage wilfully choose to portray the actions described therein otherwise? Why would this scripture about how God deliberately chose to go about things, sit uncomfortably? What would be the reasoning behind that?

A suitable helper

The very interesting and illuminating account of the creation of the first man and woman is described in Genesis 2: 4-25. When God created the earth and all that is in it, he looked at what he had created and proclaimed it *was good*. The only time God looked at one of his creations and proclaimed it was not good was after he had created the first man, Adam, and gave him the task of taking care of the Garden of Eden which God had planted '*in the East*'[3], instructing him not to eat from the tree of the knowledge of good and evil[4]:

> '*God declared, "It is not good for man to be alone. I will make a suitable helper for him*"'[5]

God then gave Adam the task of naming the animals. How clever and deliberate of God to have Adam go through this exercise. We are told that God brought the animals to Adam '*to see what he would name them*'.[6] In observing and learning more about these other living creatures, so that he could name them, Adam would have come to the realisation that none of the animals were like him in function, purpose or characteristics - they could not be in community and common purpose with him, in the way that he *needed* as a human being. How clever and deliberate of God indeed. We read in Genesis 2: 20 that among all the living creatures no '*suitable helper*' could be found[7].

Various bible translations provide additional translations for this term *suitable helper*, including, '*a helper fit for him*' (RSV), '*a helper as his partner*' (NRSVA), '*a helper comparable to him*' (NKJ), and '*a helper as his counterpart*' (YLT).

We know that God is not referring here to the man being lonely, and needing a companion whose main or only role is to be his biggest cheerleader to meet and support his emotional, relational or therapeutic needs. God says he will make him a *helper* for the task and responsibility that God had in mind. Not just any helper, but a suitable, comparable partner and counterpart, since none such needed help could be found among any of the other living creatures God created. These creatures were not created equal to the man and thus were not up to par for the task. The man, the only being created in God's image at that point, was alone and needed suitable help.

God declared that a world without such a suitable helper was *not good*. God declared that the world, without the woman and the particular capability she brought to the task, was not good. God's creation purposes for humankind could not be fulfilled without the capable participation of the woman, God's female image bearer.

And when he had fashioned the woman in his image he brought the woman to the man, just as he had done with the animals. God presented his final creation to the man to be his suitable helper. Adam, having been acquainted with all the other living creatures that God had brought to him, confirms that this woman whom God brings to him, unlike the animals, is created the same as him – bone of his bones and flesh of his flesh[8]. His suitable helper. And for this reason, we are then told in Genesis 2: 24, '*a man leaves his father and mother and is united to his wife, and they become one flesh*'.

And when God had created them, male and female in his image, he didn't just say it is good, he said '*it is very good*'.[9] God instructed *them*, the man and the woman, to rule over all living creatures, and to subdue the *earth* (not just the Garden of Eden as instructed to Adam)[10] and to have dominion over it. And then God rested. Creation was complete.

What's in a word?

So what does suitable helper mean? The Hebrew word *helper* that is used in the text is *ezer* (עֵזֶר)[11], which means *someone who saves* (*rescues another in need*). This word *ezer* appears twenty-one times in the Old Testament. It's used twice in relation to the first woman[12]. It's used three times in relation to nations to whom Israel appealed for military aid[13]. In most of the cases it's used in the bible, sixteen times in fact, it's actually used in reference to God himself as a helper[14], the God who saves.

This is a weighty word indeed. As is clear in the Hebrew meaning of the word *ezer*, it does not suggest a helper as a servant or as an assistant. This is not a passive role. Instead it denotes a vital and powerful kind of help. What God had intended was to make a partner for the man who would in every way correspond to him. A partner of strength and competence. An ally. A woman of valour. A warrior woman. The kind of suitable and comparable help needed for the achievement of God's earthly mandate.

In God's non-hierarchical design for humankind, his intention was not for the creation of the woman as a backup or support act for the man. She too, created in the image of the triune God, had to take up the mantle of the dominion mandate. The male and female image bearers bring these two expressions of God to this same given calling. All are needed for the full, powerful fulfilment of the commission from God.

The call of the woman is one of strength, competence, power and purpose and it is vital and necessary to the fulfilment of God's earthly mandate.

Yet when *ezer* is applied in attempts to make meaning of this creation event in Genesis, its meaning has usually been diminished to fit traditional and cultural views of women's role in society. The common application has suggested a more passive support role, and taken to mean a hierarchical relating between the woman and the man. In practice within the church, the expression of God brought by the female image bearer is often largely used to denote subservience in the exercise of women's calling in God's kingdom mandate.

Yet nowhere in the creation story is there any suggestion that the various characteristics of God's image, male and female, equate to the woman's calling being one that is secondary or subservient to that of the man. The only hierarchical relationship referenced in the creation story was the instruction for the man and woman to rule over the animals and other living creatures[15]. As we can see from the account of creation, and the use of the word *ezer* in reference to God himself (what an incredible endorsement of women by God), God's intention was so much more than what culture and tradition, including religious tradition, in a fallen world has hitherto seemingly been comfortable with.

Generational mandate

In the biblical creation story in Genesis 2: 4-25 the bible tells us that God first created the man, Adam, and then he fashioned the first woman, Eve, from the body (the side or rib) of Adam. However, we see in Genesis 3:20 the great unifying act by God when he confers on Eve the unique ability to bare children. Therefore, although the first woman was fashioned from the body of the man, henceforth all human beings on this earth, male and female, would come forth from the body of a woman – a position of interdependence in which ultimately '*in the Lord woman is not independent of man, nor is man independent of woman*'[16].

As part of the fulfilment of the mandate to be fruitful and multiply, men and women when coming together intimately will produce the seed for human life. God has nevertheless bestowed uniquely on women the privilege to partner with him in this creative bringing forth of human life – to carry and birth all new living human beings, and therefore all nations, on this earth.

Adam's insight into this extraordinary role that is bestowed on women within God's expansive generational mandate is shown when Adam names the woman Eve, meaning 'life' or 'the living'. He alludes to an elevated role as the mother of *all living*, rather than naming and describing her in a lesser support role as the bearer of his children.

> '*The man (Adam) called his wife Eve, because she was the mother of all living.*'[17]

What an awesome privilege of women to be Eve, the mothers of all living, the mothers of all nations.

These scriptures of God's creation in Genesis demonstrate that God's calling and purpose for women is one of significance, influence and with multi-generational kingdom impact.

CHAPTER 2

The Fall

In Genesis 2:17 God instructed Adam not to eat from the tree of the knowledge of good and evil in the Garden of Eden. This was prior to the creation of Eve. Eve we presume received this information second hand from Adam. The serpent (Satan) craftily then challenged Eve about this instruction from God, asking her '*Did God really say, "You must not eat from any tree in the garden?"*'[1] Eve is deceived by Satan into believing that eating from the tree of the knowledge of good and evil will bring her increased wisdom. Instead of conferring with Adam regarding what the serpent was saying and what God had instructed him, she believed Satan's lies and chose to eat from the tree. She also gave some to Adam, whom we are told '*was with her*'[2] when this incident with the serpent occurred. Adam, who should have known better as he had full knowledge of God's direct instructions to him, chose to forego his responsibility and also ate the fruit. Adam and Eve rebelled against God's instructions. They both ate the fruit from the tree, and the curse of sin entered the world as a result.

God's intention for the man and the woman was for a vital, powerful partnership in the fulfilment of God's mandate on earth. But then sin, death and brokenness entered the world.

Let's unpack this and examine how this consequently affects women in their calling on earth.

A hostile battle

The first change that we see affecting the woman's earthly mandate and call is in the curse God declares on Satan in Genesis 3: 15,

> '*And I will put enmity between you and the woman, and between her seed and your seed; he will crush your head, and you will strike his heel.*'

The first messianic prophecy in the Bible about the coming of Christ is declared here by God himself as an act of restoring what has been destroyed through the Fall - the seed of the woman, Jesus Christ, will crush Satan's head.

And by virtue of this, right there in the Garden of Eden, the significant role and calling of a woman, Mary of Nazareth, as the mother of Jesus Christ is sealed.

God also declares here in this moment an action and intention that he himself puts in place, as part of the curse he places on Satan: '*I will put enmity between you and the woman*'.

It is notable in Genesis 3: 15 how the first messianic prophecy about the coming battle between Jesus Christ and Satan is framed together with the role of the woman in that spiritual battle of the ages against Satan, and in God's redemption story.

God declares that going forward the reality of life in a fallen world will be marked by a state of active opposition and hostility between the woman and Satan.

There are two ways we are to understand this.

Firstly, as a curse *on Satan* God places women on the frontline of an active, direct battle against the ruler of this world. *God places women here in a significant role in God's kingdom victory*.

Women are a powerful weapon that God uses in the spiritual battle against Satan, so that Satan is crushed and God's kingdom comes on earth.

Secondly, because Satan knows this, women will as a result experience the uniquely directed hostility of Satan. The female image bearer of God will come under ongoing targeted onslaught from the devil and his seed with the aim of reducing the woman's power and impact in the spiritual battle for God's kingdom.

Let that sink in.

In the context of what we know of history and the status of women even today, let it truly sink in. It is no wonder that throughout human history Satan has worked so particularly hard to diminish the identity, role and legitimacy of women both spiritually and societally, to reduce their power.

Satan has continued in his schemes and tactics to reduce and subjugate women and continue his lie uttered in the Garden of Eden, '*Did God really say.....?*' Did God really say that you are an ezer? Did God really say that he gives you dominion authority over the earth? Did God really say you are to go forth, be fruitful and multiply in partnership with men? Did God really say that he is placing you at the forefront of the battle against Satan, for his kingdom? Did God really say that he bestows all spiritual gifts on you and commands you to run your race full out?

When women, together with men, operate in the full spiritual power God intended for them, and in the full knowledge of who they are in Christ, what they would birth would result in Satan's crushing, in his destruction. And he knows it. The woman and her seed will crush Satan and his seed's head. Her seed's heel may be bruised in the battle, but Satan is crushed. The victory is certain.

Hierarchy in marital relationship

The second change affecting women's mandate and calling that we see after the Fall is when God says to the woman, '*Your desire will be for your husband, and he will rule over you*' [3].

God *describes* here how henceforth, for generations to come, the marital partnership between husband and wife is adversely affected by the entrance of sin. The fact that a husband's rule or dominance over his wife is declared for the first time here, post sin in a now fallen world, reiterates again that this gender hierarchy was not in existence before when God created the man and the woman, and is not understood to have been part of the original life God intended and desired for women or men.

The hierarchical relating between the first husband and wife is the consequence of a fallen human nature and a broken world, and the curse of sin and death that had entered the world. It is not prescriptive of an ideal or desired way of being for those who are co-heirs with Christ himself. Just as we do not consider painful childbirth as a desired ideal for women and take measures to relieve this pain, neither do we consider it only biblical when a man earns his living and sustains his family solely '*by the sweat of (his) brow*' painfully toiling the ground in manual agricultural work, rather than through less labor intensive intellectual and creative pursuits such as the arts or political activism. These are two outcomes of sin entering the world that are also described in the same texts here in Genesis[4]. If we consider the hierarchy between men and women as a prescriptive principle for desired biblical living, then we need to apply the same logic to these other consequences of the Fall also listed in the very same biblical passage.

Genesis 3:16 does not describe the *rule* of *all* men over *all* women in society either. It refers to the fallen dynamic in the marital relationship between the husband and wife. It is incredible then that following this episode in the Garden of Eden, widespread subjugation of women permeated our wider society and culture throughout history. You see, when sin entered the world not only did this break the man and woman's intimate fellowship with God, it also broke the fellowship they once had with each other as God's image bearers. Men and women have sadly suffered the destructive consequences ever since. It has resulted in a pervasive broken state of living for both men and women when they do not walk in harmonious partnership, together reflecting the full image of God.[5]

'Headship' that is exercised as the authoritative dominance or control of a man over a woman in marriage, as opposed to the existence of respectful partnership and mutuality, is unlikely to stay within the confines of a marriage or even the nuclear household. The dynamics and ways of relating we tolerate and espouse in the home, we will most likely also understand and practice as acceptable or permissible elsewhere, outside of the home. And what children observe, understand and emulate in their homes when they grow up, is what they consequently understand about the roles and value of men and women in general.

What is modelled and normalised in the home shapes how we operate in the world in general, and what we willingly and actively defend and advocate for in the public spaces and in the communities in which we live and serve.

And when a woman buys into the lies of Satan about her rightful identity in God, and does not know who she truly is and what she is made for, she will be tempted to strive in order to make sense of this outside of this divine design and purpose – comparing and seeking the approval and acceptance of others (including the desire for her husband's approval and acceptance) in order to be validated.

CHAPTER 3

A World out of Balance

And boy oh boy, has history not born witness to the consequences of these very things! From the first humans on earth to the multiplied nations across the globe, what we've seen historically is not just a broken relational power dynamic between husband and wife within the marital home, but rather there has also been a cultural social system of the dominance of men over women who are not their wives or even their relatives within the larger structure of society outside the home.

The human social structures and norms that were developed and that have evolved over time were likely for all intents and purposes initially founded on well-intentioned interest in the protection and preservation of communities and their members. However, the on-the-ground execution of these structures and norms has historically been unbalanced, leading to a disadvantageous, disempowered and sometimes even destructive state of being for women and girls in many communities.

> ***The battle of women throughout the ages has been one marked by a suffering for equal value, rightful identity and common purpose.***

For generations women did not have a seat at the table where fundamental decisions, plans and resolutions were being made that affect them, their lives and their children's lives – this includes developed nations with a majority Christian population.

The right to an education[1]

Women have faced thousands of years of negative opinion regarding stereotypes of women's intellectual inferiority, their perceived role in society, and whether it was wise, necessary or even safe for them to be educated and professionally trained. In ancient times up until medieval times, in a few societies access to some studies was only available to select upper class or noble women. During the Renaissance and early modern period in Europe, 1 Timothy 2: 11-12 was widely used to oppose education for women, and teaching by women[2]. Knowledge is power and women's restriction and exclusion from an education and professional training came hand in hand with restricted access to certain marketplace professions and creative pursuits (art, music, literature) where they could contribute their voice, creative ideas, intellect and abilities, and exercise their God-given gifts and talents.

The first woman graduated from the University of Bologna in 1237, but female enrolment in colleges and universities remained an exception. It wasn't until the Reformation in the 16th century that mandatory education of both boys *and* girls was supported. From the second half of the 19th century onwards enrolment of women in colleges and universities grew, with a huge increase in these numbers in the 1960's and 1970's as the societal mindset shifted to accept women as scholars, rather than just the need to be educated to be good mothers. Women now make up the majority of scholars at higher education institutions in developed nations, but leading positions at these institutions remain largely male-occupied. In many low-income countries today there remains a sizeable disparity with less girls than boys being educated.

The right to vote[3]

If ever there was a right that is integral to the effective and appropriate execution of our mandate to rule and have dominion over the earth, it is the right to vote. And yet this is a relatively recent privilege afforded to women. This lack of the right to vote severely limited women's say in who represents their and their children's interests in local and national government. New Zealand was the first nation to grant women the right to vote in 1893. In most other countries, women did not have the right to vote until much later in the 20th century after the Second World War. It may come as a surprise to some that Switzerland only granted women the right to vote in federal elections in 1971, while women were not allowed to vote in its many local state elections till the late 1980's, with the last state in Switzerland to allow women to vote was in 1991. Saudia Arabia is the most recent nation in 2015 to allow women to vote and run for office. In many countries, women of color and indigenous women didn't get the right to vote until decades after white women.

The right to own property and land[4]

The first records of women being able to acquire, own and dispose of property in their own name was in ancient Egypt (3100 BCE and after). Historically, women were largely not allowed to inherit property (see the story of Zelophehad's daughters later in this book to see how such inheritance laws were adapted for the Jewish people). It wasn't until the 800's that Anglo-Saxon laws allowed women in Europe to own their own property before and after marriage. In 1850 Iceland became the first country to institute unconditional equal inheritance rights for women. And yet today, in some parts of the world women still cannot legally own or control land. In half of the world's countries, women are still unable to assert equal land and property rights, despite some legal protections, due to persistent discriminatory social norms and practices, weak implementation of policies and lack of political will. This hampers women's economic status and opportunities to overcome poverty.

Nowhere is this pervasive issue more significant today than in agriculture and farming. Women make up a substantial percentage (20% - 48%) of the worldwide agricultural labor force today, yet only 5% - 18% are land owners[5]. Data shows that gender-specific obstacles put female farmers at a significant disadvantage - lack of access to land, financing, markets, agricultural training and education, suitable working conditions and equal treatment[6]. Research suggests that if female farmers in developing countries had the same access to these resources as men, the production of their farms would increase by up to 30%, in turn increasing their country's agricultural production by up to 4%, and decreasing the number of hungry people by 12%[7]. Women's property and land ownership provides increased income and security, and is linked to better nutrition and higher educational attainment for girls and women[8].

Women's diminished role in the dominion mandate

All these cultural and societal restrictions have historically reduced women's agency and denied women equivalent opportunity to have their voices heard and to make a difference in a fundamental way outside the home and at the highest levels of society. It severely restricted their ability to competently and completely fulfil their dominion mandate in the world.

Where women have made such intellectual and cultural contributions to the evolution of humanity and stewardship of the earth, their contributions have largely gone unacknowledged in the annals of recorded history. Women have been largely unseen and unremembered. Invisible.

People of color have historically also experienced such societal limitations and exclusions as a result of systemic and structural racism. So particularly for women of color, for generations this has been a double whammy of gender and race based discrimination and disadvantage.

A key moral challenge for this generation remains the inequity between the male and female image bearers of God, where the lives of women and girls continue to be undervalued based on their gender. The statistics on the epidemic violence against women and girls globally are heartbreaking.

- There has been more gender-based killings of girls in any one decade than people were killed in all the genocides of the twentieth century. More girls have been killed in such gender-based killing in the last five to six decades, than all the men killed in all the wars of the twentieth century combined. It is estimated that annually at least 2 million girls disappear worldwide[9].
- Much of this gender-based killing is perpetrated inside the family. More than half (58%) of women intentionally killed in 2017 were killed by intimate partners or family members[10]. This means that 137 women across the world are intentionally killed by a member of their own family every day. At least 5000 honor killings occur globally each year[11].
- About 1 in 3 (35%) of women have experienced sexual and physical violence in their lifetime[12], most at the hands of an intimate partner. Women aged 15-44 are more at risk from rape and domestic violence than from war, cancer, malaria and car accidents[13]. Pentagon data from 2013 showed that female soldiers serving in Iraq or Afghanistan were more likely to be raped by a comrade than killed by an enemy[14].
- More than 200 million girls and women alive today in 30 countries have experienced female genital mutilation (FGM)[15].
- Such gender-based violence prevents women from fully participating in society and has negative physical and mental consequences for women as well as their families, the community and a nation at large.

When God created us on the 6th day he intended for males and females together to take stewardship responsibility in the dominion mandate. It is judicious to acknowledge here that because of our biophysical differences, the physicality of males can be more advantageous for some task requirements. Similarly, one must acknowledge that not all men or women are homogenous groups, thus rendering it difficult to apply blanket rationalisations for gender-based role selection and exclusion. Though we have seen progress globally in recent decades, women's representation and access to similar opportunities as men to contribute to human society remains unbalanced still.

- 104 out of 189 economies assessed in 2018 still have laws preventing women from working in specific jobs. In 18 global economies husbands can legally prevent their wives from working[16].
- In many families today, both parents work in formal or paid employment, and few can afford not to. However, women are paid on average an estimated 23% less than men worldwide[17] (this varies across nations).
- In addition, women still bear a disproportionate caring responsibility for children, the sick and elderly family members, even in two-income households. Women spend almost 3 times more time than men on unpaid care and domestic work (i.e. women do 75% of the world's unpaid care work), irrespective of the proportion of household income they bring in[18].
- The time spent on domestic chores is most equal by gender for single men and women. When women start to cohabit, their time spent on domestic chores increases, while men's goes down, regardless of employment status[19].
- And when all work is considered, both paid and unpaid, women are found to work longer hours than men and enjoy less leisure time[20]. The COVID lockdown restrictions shone a spotlight on this burden that is carried by women.

- Women remain underrepresented among business and political leaders. There were only 4 women among the 850 international delegates who signed the founding document of the United Nations, the UN Charter, in 1945. 10% of Fortune 500 CEOs are women[21]. Women remain a small minority among leaders of countries (heads of state or government) and just 25% of national parliamentary members worldwide are women[22].

Consequences of exclusion and underrepresentation

We have lived in a world with the traditional ideological belief that the needs and perspectives of men, who have historically had exclusive access to seats at the decision-making table, are the universal standard and are representative of humans overall. This historic gender underrepresentation and the exclusion of women from contributing in a pivotal way to humanity and the creation of its societal norms (from car design to urban planning or medical treatments), has however had consequences. In Caroline Criado Perez's revealing data packed book, Invisible Women[23], we see that this has resulted in:

- a male bias (however unintended it may be) with regards to what products, policies, laws, services or government budgetary spending are prioritised, and
- that such policies, products, laws and services that are designed and produced are often lacking, inappropriate or even unsafe for women and girls, putting their health and lives at risk (e.g., women are 47% more likely to suffer severe injuries in car crashes because the safety features are designed to be suitable for men).

We operate in a state of incompleteness when male and female image bearers do not operate in the world in equitable partnership. Diversity of thought, perception and experience enrich the ideas, insights and outcomes generated through such sharing and collaboration - a synergy of the strengths that men and women bring, to produce a combined impact that is greater than the sum of their separate individual effects. And so, when we are shaping and transforming a society that is meant to work for everyone, we need women at the table too. Equivalent access and space for both men and women's voices and perspectives at all levels is critical.

Women's positive impact

We know of course from research data that the contribution of women bears much fruit and enriches the impact and outcomes of mixed gender teams and partnerships. For instance, data shows that women are great for business and leadership. There is a positive correlation between women in senior leadership teams and a company's performance and economic returns[24]. Companies with 3 or more female directors on their boards generate 35% higher return on equity than those that do not[25].

How much more of an impact can we thus make in all spheres of society, in the marketplace and at the highest levels – business, education, government, media, sports, science and technology, the environment, arts and entertainment - when righteous men and women come together to add value and make a difference? Just imagine that. The calling of women within all spheres of society, and in the shaping of that society and its norms, is vital.

Before you find yourself dissociating from the data and assuming these are not relevant to you personally, ascribing these to cultural paradigms that are outside of the core matters or issues at hand for you today – think again. God has always had a global perspective. God cares about all his children, no matter where they are placed across the earth. His imprint, identity and mandate is on all his children, and the lived experiences of women and girls across the world matters to God. If we believe that women are made in the image of God then we should honestly evaluate all cultural and social issues through that lens. No one wins when women, and the image of God that is reflected in women, are devalued.

Since the Fall in Genesis 3, God had a redemptive plan of restoration and victory over Satan, sin and death[26]. Despite this prejudicial picture of human history, the Bible is full of examples of how God used women in extraordinary ways, shedding an illuminating spotlight on God's own agenda for women in his mission on earth. The following chapters of this book examine these biblical examples.

PART 2
Women's Calling Throughout the Scriptures

CHAPTER 4

The Role of Women in the Old Testament

As disciples we walk in the company of the godly men and women who had gone before, both named and unnamed. Role models on whose shoulders we now stand. Though the cultural, societal, legal and religious norms limited women in a way it did not men, nonetheless we do see in the Old Testament that women participated in various societal activities and roles.

Women were included when the Mosaic covenant was instituted[1]. They were present at Joshua's reading of the Torah to Israel[2] and at public readings of the scriptures on the Feast of the Tabernacles[3]. Women prayed in the temple[4], played music and worshipped in the sanctuary[5] and sang and danced in religious processions. They engaged in manual labor[6] and in substantive occupations in commerce and real estate as seen in the commendation of the Proverbs 31 woman[7].

Though many stories of women are likely untold or lost to history, the Old Testament does indeed contain testimonies of women from diverse backgrounds who have exercised their faith and calling with power and impact. Women of courage and wisdom whose actions and lives shaped the fate of tribes, cities and nations, like the diverse women mentioned below.

- ***Rachel and Leah***[8] were sisters who were married to Jacob and from whom the twelve tribes of the House of Israel was built. In a cultural time when it was very much a man's world, they are two of the five women mentioned in the Old Testament who were given burials of honor (the other three women being Sarah, Rebekah and Rebekah's nurse[9]).

- ***Miriam***[10] was the sister of Moses and Aaron. Together with Moses' mother she helped to preserve his life as a baby. When God brought the Israelites out of Egypt to freedom, Miriam played a significant leading role as a prophet during this exodus journey, as recognised in Micah 6: 4 (NLT), '*For I brought you out of Egypt and redeemed you from slavery. I sent Moses, Aaron and Miriam to help you*'. Her prophetic songs are included as part of biblical scripture. She is one of the few women listed among the male descendants in the Mosaic census of the Israelite clans, alongside her brothers Moses and Aaron.

- ***Sarah***[11] was the wife of Abraham who, despite her advanced age, through faith bore her son Isaac and became the mother of nations. She was given a burial of honor. In the New Testament scriptures, she is one of the two women commended in the great cloud of witnesses as an example of great faith (the other woman is Rahab).

- ***Hagar***[12] was the Egyptian slave of Abraham and Sarah who bore Abraham the son, Ishmael. As a slave she had no social status, but is recorded in the bible as the first person in scripture to be visited by an angel and the only person in scripture to give God a name - El Roi, 'the God who sees me'. God saw and reached down to this desperate woman and gave her a similar promise as that given to Abraham: He will make her son Ishmael into a great nation, and her descendants will be increased so much that they will be too numerous to count.

- ***Deborah***[13] was a married, multi-gifted woman who was a poet, prophet, military leader and the fifth judge of Israel, rising to national civic and spiritual leadership at a time when there were no kings. She was a strong, inspiring leader who led the Israelites with authority and wisdom. Deborah commanded such respect for her leadership, faith and courage that when she called on the war leader Barak to take the field against the oppressor Sisera, he would only agree if she went onto the battlefield with him and the all-male army. She did and they won the battle. She is a great example of a strong woman who took charge.

In a definitive statement she declared: '*Villagers in Israel would not fight; they held back until I, Deborah, arose, until I arose, a Mother in Israel.*' Yet, as far as we know, Deborah had no biological children. Nothing is known of her husband, except his name. Deborah uses the term *Mother* as a term of Leadership - leadership through a woman's lens and perspective, leadership through a woman's experience and understanding, leadership with a woman's wisdom, leadership with an emphasis on the unique female characteristics she brings to that position and its responsibilities. Deborah's story challenges us to expand our preconceived ideas about how God would use us – irrespective of our marital or parental status – to lead and mentor a generation in wisdom and righteousness.

- ***Jael***[14] was a housewife married to Heber the Kenite, and who was part of the same story with Deborah. She offered the oppressor Sisera shelter after he fled from the complete massacre of his troops by the army Deborah led on the battlefield. When Sisera was asleep, Jael killed him by driving a tent peg through his temple (her husband's whereabouts during this course of events is unrecorded). Jael was courageous and took control of the situation. Like Deborah, she played a decisive role in Israel's victory.

- ***Huldah***[15] was a married prophet whose standing and powerful reputation led to King Josiah consulting her instead of the renowned prophets Jeremiah and Zephaniah. She was authoritative and fearless in delivering a challenging prophetic message. Huldah used her spiritual gift to uniquely serve a king and an entire nation. Her prophetic message and the public reading of the law unveiled the future of a nation, and brought about revival and reforms.

- ***Isaiah's wife***[16] was herself a prophet, and is recognised as such by the prophet Isaiah himself.

- ***Esther***[17] was an orphan who married the King of Persia. The king's minister, Haman, had the king issue a royal decree ordering the destruction of the Jews. God had providentially placed Esther in a key position of influence to affect the destiny of God's people. She courageously stepped into her calling, risking her life, and faced the king for the deliverance of her people. She intentionally utilised her position as Queen to avert a genocide of the Jews. The book of Esther is named after her.

- ***Jehosheba***[18]. When Jehoram, the son and heir to King Jehoshaphat, was killed, his grandmother Athaliah started killing all the other potential heirs so that she herself could become ruler. Athaliah's own daughter, Jehosheba, took and hid her infant nephew, Joash, for six years until he reached the age of seven and was then crowned as king. Her brave and defiant action ensured that the line of David was preserved.

- ***Hannah***[19] was one of the two wives of Elkanah. She was barren for many years but her steadfast faith and unceasing prayer for a child was rewarded. She dedicated her son Samuel back to God, and he, like Deborah, became a prophet and judge over Israel. Samuel played a key role in the transition from judges to kings in Israel, and was tasked with anointing Saul and David as kings. David was one of the greatest rulers through whose lineage Jesus would come. Hannah's prayer became part of the biblical scriptures.

- ***Abigail***[20] was an Israelite woman who was married to Nabal, a rich man of poor character. While her husband disrespected David, she recognised God's hand on David. She took decisive action to meet with David without her husband, and with humility and diplomacy counselled him (thus preventing a violent attack and bloodshed), and prophesied David's kingship over Israel. After the death of Nabal she became one of David's wives who is actually named in the Bible. She is affirmed in the scriptures for her initiative, wisdom and courage.

- ***The woman of Abel***[21]**.** King David faced a serious rebellion led by a man named Sheba. David's army commander, Joab, besieged the city of Abel Beth Maacah in which Sheba had taken refuge. As Joab's army were battering the city wall to bring it down, an unnamed wise woman of that city determined what needed to be done to save this crucial, ancient city and took charge of the situation. She called out to Joab, counselled him and promised that Sheba's head will be handed over to Joab in exchange for the preservation of the city. She then advised the people of the city who were all convinced by her, had Sheba killed, threw his head to Joab and thus saved their city - all at the leading and influence of this unnamed wise woman.

- ***The Daughters of Zelophehad***[22] requested and received their father's estate in a time when inequality existed between daughters and sons, and property was only inherited by male heirs. Their father had no sons and had passed away, and they were unmarried at the time. They made a bold decision to go to the tent of meeting where Moses, Eleazar the priest and all the male leaders and elders had assembled, and boldly spoke in front of them seeking justice for themselves – the first such instance by women recorded the bible. They petitioned Moses and the elders for their right to be considered their father's legal heirs and to inherit his property rights. Their example of female leadership came at a time and place when women and children were not considered significant to even be counted.

Not knowing what to do as the inheritance law made no such provision for women, Moses consulted God, who declared that the women were right. As a result of their landmark legal case the laws of inheritance were rewritten, as recorded later in the book of Numbers[23]. (Consequentially in the book of Job[24] after Job's wealth was restored, we read that he granted his daughters an inheritance along with their brothers). Zelophehad's daughters were thus included by name among the males in the Mosaic census of the Israelite clans[25]. Their story reminds us that we all belong at God's table.

And then of course there are also the four Old Testament women, who together with Mary the mother of Jesus, are mentioned alongside the Jewish male ancestors in the legal hereditary genealogy of Jesus[26]:

- ***Tamar***[27] was twice widowed and childless in a society and culture in which women were vulnerable. She tricked her father-in-law into impregnating her, in order to gain the societal and legal covering he should have afforded her but had reneged on. She took huge risks and showed incredible courage and resourcefulness in her determination to get justice, as it was understood in the society at that time. So much so that when her actions and identity were revealed her father-in-law Judah declared: '*She is more righteous than I*'. Tamar is recognized in scripture as an integral figure in the generational plans of God.

- ***Rahab***[28] was an Amorite prostitute who, having understood God's sovereignty, played her part in enabling the Israelites' victory over Jericho and entry into the Promised Land by shielding two Jewish spies. She later married one of Joshua's spies, Salmon, and thus became an ancestor in David's and Jesus' lineage. She is considered righteous for her works and is commended in the great cloud of witnesses as an example of great faith (alongside Sarah).

- ***Ruth***[29] was a faithful and determined Moabite convert and immigrant widow who rose from obscurity to marry Boaz, her kinsman redeemer, and become an ancestor of Jesus in the line of David. The book of Ruth in the bible is named after her. Her story provides a shadow of gentiles who would be saved by a Kinsman Redeemer, Jesus Christ.

- ***Bathsheba***[30] was Uriah's wife whom David summoned and impregnated. She was redeemed by God and became the mother of Solomon. Solomon followed his father David as King and was known for his leadership and wisdom. Bathsheba was a woman who endured much suffering and overcame, consequently rising in honor and influence in the royal court with both King David and King Solomon.

- ***Mary***[31] was the mother of Jesus whose role was predicted at the Fall in Genesis 3 in the first messianic prophecy and in messianic prophecies throughout the Old Testament, and she's also mentioned in the New Testament. She was a woman who accepted God's calling on her life to carry, birth and raise the Messiah at potentially great personal cost. Mary's Song is part of the biblical scriptures. She remained a steadfast disciple throughout her life, even after Jesus' death and the birth of the new Christian church.

What makes the inclusion of these five women even more extraordinary is the fact that they are outside of our normal understanding of whom God would choose, and how he would accomplish his purposes (admittedly the same could be said of many of the flawed and imperfect men providentially included in Jesus' genealogy). At least two of these women were Gentiles. Tamar posed as a prostitute to trick her father-in-law into impregnating her, to bring herself and her children into the familial lineage. Rahab was a prostitute. Ruth was a foreign widow who was viewed as undesirable by her deceased husband's closest family relative who should have married her. Bathsheba was a married woman forced into adultery by David. Mary, though a virgin, was nonetheless a woman who found herself pregnant before her marriage ceremony.

Women shaping history

Just to remind ourselves again of some highlights from the stories of these Old Testament women: two have books of the Bible named after them (Ruth and Esther), several spoke and/or wrote words that became scripture (Miriam, Deborah, Hannah and Mary the mother of Jesus), five were given burials of honor (Leah, Rachel, Sarah, Rebekah and Rebekah's nurse), two are mentioned among the saints as examples of people with great faith (Sarah and Rahab), several were recognized as prophets (including Miriam, Deborah, Hannah, Huldah and Isaiah's wife), one was a national civic and spiritual leader over the nation of Israel (Deborah), and five are included in the genealogy of Jesus.

And these are only the few stories selected for this book! The Old Testament contains testimonies of more women, both named and unnamed.

You see, God will not be thwarted[32]. When women courageously and boldly dare to believe in a God who has called them to something significant in their generation, irrespective of what the existent social or cultural paradigms would deem acceptable or possible, God will have his way. And he *will* and does use women in significant ways for his kingdom.

The Old Testament authors recognized the hand of God in elevating and using women in shaping the destiny that God has for his people, beyond the societal restrictions and cultural understanding of women's roles. These stories, including Deborah's leadership over men, are not recorded as examples of women stepping out of line, not staying in their lanes and going against an understood biblical order for the gender roles of women and men. Rather, the bible authors have intentionally included, acknowledged and highlighted these women's testimonies as ones to be positively noted, celebrated and honored as key narratives in God's story – a deliberate inclusion in scriptures which will go on to instruct generations of God's people henceforth.

The authors recognised how God gave women an integral role in his generational kingdom purposes and in the redemption story of the promised Messiah. In Ruth 4:11-12 we read,

> '*Then the elders and all the people at the gate said,* "*We are witnesses. May the Lord make the woman who is coming into your home like Rachel and Leah, who together built up the family of Israel. May you have standing in Ephrathah and be famous in Bethlehem. Through the offspring the Lord gives you by this young woman, may your family be like that of Perez, whom Tamar bore to Judah*"'.

Through these Old Testament examples we can see that God has always exercised and demonstrated a purpose and calling for women that is one of significance and agency and with multi-generational kingdom impact. The liberated and empowered way in which God would use and view women, his female image bearers, is not a new dispensation evidenced only in the New Testament. God is not mankind that he should lie. His promises remain. He is the same yesterday, today and forever[33]. These positively conveyed Old Testament testimonies demonstrate that God does not abide by our human rules and norms. They attest instead to God's understanding of women's true identity in him and the mandate and purpose he has had for women and men alike since the 6th day of Creation.

To underscore the significance of this, many of these Old Testament women are in fact not only mentioned in the Old Testament but are also referred to again in the New Testament.

CHAPTER 5

Jesus and the Calling of Women

By the time of the 1st century during Jesus' time on earth, women's social standing and freedoms had changed from those enjoyed by women in Old Testament times. Women were understood to be of the same status as their husband's other possessions, such as his cattle or his property. It was not deemed necessary for them to learn to read so that they could study the scriptures for themselves. Women and men were separated in public and religious life. Women could go to the temple, but were not allowed to participate in public prayer at the temple, and had to remain confined to the women's court of the temple (no records of a separate women's court is found in biblical descriptions of Solomon's temple). Respectable women were mostly expected to remain within the confines of their homes - women were neither to be seen nor heard. A woman's primary roles and duty was that of wife and mother. The reasons for this deterioration in women's roles and the change in their societal status is not entirely known. It is thought that the Jewish religious leaders who assimilated these cultural norms were likely influenced by similar Greek schools of thought[1].

Jesus honored women in the way the religious leaders and cultural norms of the day did not. In love, he challenged the understanding of women's primary role as wives and mothers[2] and shattered the restricted status of 1st century women. Jesus modelled a better way - a just, restorative social agenda affirming women's God-ordained identity and mandate, and how men and women are to operate together in the fulfilment of that mutual mandate.

At a time when women were treated as second class citizens, women mattered with Jesus. He broke down the patriarchal bias of the culture and tasked women with roles and activities that would have been understood to be the privilege of men. He also broke through a number of taboos with regards to interactions between men and women. Women stood before him with dignity and on their own merit, both publicly and in the home. He spoke directly to women, modelling in the natural the spiritual notion that all, including women, have direct access to God.

He included women. He taught them. He celebrated them. He *saw* them. He did not side line them or diminish their place in the community of believers. Women were visible with Jesus.

Let's examine six biblical examples where Jesus publicly demonstrated the honor and value he conferred on women, and the freedom to which he called them.

The woman caught in adultery[3]

A woman caught in adultery was brought before Jesus by a group of Pharisees and teachers of the law, to be publicly shamed, with the man involved in this adultery nowhere to be seen. Jesus doodled with his finger in the sand, remaining poignantly silent and refusing to condemn her. This incident becomes one of the most teachable moments in the scriptures – it exposed the men's biases regarding the sin of adultery by both males and females, and highlighted how little care they actually had for true justice.

These religious leaders displayed a biased cultural attitude and viewpoint that was no different to that which was found outside the temple and synagogue walls in the secular society of that day. But Jesus was not afraid to act counter to their cultural and religious understanding, and chose a higher way. When her accusers left one by one, Jesus spoke to the woman with words of grace and truth, illustrating the combination of justice and mercy in his salvation.

The woman healed on a Sabbath[4]

Jesus noticed a woman in the synagogue who'd been crippled and bent over for 18 years. He called her to the front where he was teaching, publicly declared her free and she was healed. Jesus chastised and publicly humiliated the synagogue leader who objected to this woman's healing on a Sabbath. He stated that if they could show compassion by doing the physical work of untying their farm animals so they can drink water on a Sabbath, so much more should compassion be extended to this woman, who is as much a daughter, as they are sons, of Abraham.

Jewish men were familiar with the reference to them as 'sons of Abraham', but in rabbinical teaching no woman was ever referred as a '*daughter of Abraham*'. Hearing this spoken would have been shocking for those in the crowd. Jesus elevated a woman to a place alongside men, and thereby taught that women have an equal standing and inheritance in the promise of the covenant, just like any man. This view was also repeated by the apostle Paul when he declared that we are neither male nor female, we are all '*Abraham's seed*'[5].

Jesus *saw* this woman. He *called her forward* to a place of visibility. He *declared her free* from years of bondage even before she physically straightened up. We face the same call from Jesus today, to step into visibility and to declare our freedom from all that is stopping us from running the race full out!

The woman with the issue of blood[6]

A woman had suffered for 12 years with what we presume is a gynaecological issue of excessive bleeding. According to Levitical law[7] she was considered ceremonially unclean and would need to quarantine as anyone whom she touched would be considered unclean too. In pursuit of unsuccessful treatments for her condition, she had become broke. However when she heard

Jesus was passing through she risked going out in public, pushing through a dense crowd, having faith that she would be healed if she just touched Jesus' hem.

Jesus makes a point of calling her out publicly, and though she was trembling and afraid, he gets her to explain why she touched him, for all the crowd to hear. For Jesus it was more important for this woman to be freed from her suffering, shame and reclusive invisibility, than for any concern about social propriety and religious laws, so she could live freely with dignity like any other citizen.

The woman who anointed Jesus[8]

A woman of ill-repute heard that Jesus was dining at the house of the Pharisee, Simon. She took an alabaster jar filled with perfume and upon entering the home she stood behind Jesus, weeping. She wet his feet with her tears, wiped them with her hair, and anointed him by pouring perfume on them. A profound act of love, worship and surrender.

The religious leader scoffed and questioned Jesus' legitimacy as a prophet - he had seemingly not shown knowledge of this woman's sins, since he allowed her to do what she did. But Jesus instead pointed out how this woman's actions compared more favorably than the welcome he'd received from this religious leader, the Pharisee. Jesus publicly honored this woman's act of faith and in the presence of all those observing, forgave her sins and freed her from the shackles of her past.

The woman who sat at Jesus' feet[9]

Mary of Bethany lived with her sister Martha and her brother Lazarus. When Jesus and his disciples passed through the town of Bethany, Martha opened their house to him. While Martha occupied herself with the role and domestic tasks typically expected of women - to serve the guests - Mary instead chose to sit at Jesus' feet in the posture of a rabbinical pupil, listening and learning as he spoke and taught. This position as a pupil or disciple was usually only deemed appropriate and applicable for the men at the time and was a deeply counter cultural thing for Mary to do. Jesus afforded this woman a seat at his table like any of his male disciples and followers. When Martha asked Jesus to chastise Mary for not helping her instead, Jesus positively affirmed Mary's actions. Jesus deemed her bold choice as a woman to abide with Jesus in intimate communion, meditating on his words, as the better thing to do, more than any other concerns or works of service we may occupy ourselves with.

The same Mary of Bethany was found again at Jesus' feet after the resurrection from the dead of her brother Lazarus, where she poured expensive perfume on Jesus' feet and dried them with her hair. This was the second such act of profound love and worship by a woman recorded in the scriptures. She was chastised by the disciples, particularly Judas, for wasting such an expensive resource. However, Jesus declared that there would always be the opportunity to do good works for the poor but that they would not always have him with them. Jesus affirmed Mary's actions - she had once again prioritised and honored the presence and person of Jesus, just days before the Messiah's own death and burial.

The woman at the well[10]

Jesus engaged a Samaritan woman at a well in a conversation, in breach of the normal social etiquette for genders and the prevalent dislike between Jews and Samaritans at the time. His discourse with her, where he afforded her equal dignity and responded to her questions, is one of the longest theological discussions recorded in the bible.

Outside of his own earthly mother and family, she is the first person in the bible to whom Jesus revealed his deity and his mission on earth – a new season where believers everywhere, operating in equal status and in the power of the Spirit, irrespective of background, gender or social standing, are a powerful transformational force for social change and the ushering in of God's kingdom.

This woman's story demonstrates God's global agenda for all people across the earth. She became the first Samaritan convert and one of the greatest evangelists recorded in the bible, long before Peter or Paul started spreading the gospel to the gentiles. Many men and women in her city became believers on the strength of her testimony. She declared that Jesus was the Messiah, the *Savior of the world*, not just the Savior of the Jews - the only place recorded in the gospel of a person declaring Jesus as such. As a result of her evangelism, Jesus spent two days with the Samaritans.

In all of these women's encounters with Jesus he removed the societal shame and restrictions from them, and conferred on them worth and dignity, thereby not only restoring and empowering the individual but also society's perception of women.

The role of women in Jesus' ministry

Women were central to the ministry of Jesus. Jesus deliberately gave women foundational and primary roles in the main events of his ministry, and revealed powerful truths about himself and his mission directly to women.

Women witnessed and were involved in many firsts in Jesus' earthly ministry:

- As we read before, five women were included in the legal hereditary genealogy of Jesus[11]: Tamar, Rahab, Ruth, Bathsheba and Mary. Jewish genealogy would normally only list the male ancestors through whom legal lineage is determined.

- The first history-making announcement of Christ's incarnation, something the Jewish people were eagerly awaiting and which had been prophesied at the Fall and throughout the Old Testament scriptures, was given to women - first to Mary and then her cousin Elizabeth, the mother of John the Baptist[12].

- After Jesus was born and presented in the temple, the prophet Anna[13] blessed him. She was the first person who spoke about him publicly to all who were eagerly awaiting the redemption of God's people.

- Jesus performed his first public miracle[14] which revealed his deity and signalled the start of his messianic mission, when he turned water into wine at the wedding in Cana. This was performed at the encouragement of, and witnessed by, a woman – his mother, Mary.

- The first Samaritan convert[15] was the woman at the well. Also, the first Gentile convert was a woman – a Syrophoenician mother[16] whose child Jesus healed.

- The first person (outside of his own earthly mother and family) whom Jesus publicly told that he was the Messiah, revealing his deity and mission on earth, was to a Samaritan woman[17].

- Jesus' first theological teaching on the resurrection[18] - correlating the person of Jesus, his own resurrection from the dead and the final resurrection - was first given to a woman, Martha.

- Women were the first people who were told of Jesus' resurrection[19].

- Women were the first people to whom the resurrected Christ appeared[20].

- The risen Christ himself commissioned women to be the first public evangelists and preachers of Jesus' resurrection to others, including to the eleven disciples[21] – they were tasked with the authority and responsibility to share the gospel not just to other women, but to all. This significant detail is recorded in all four gospels.

- The only recorded witness to be present at the birth and death of Jesus Christ as well the birth of the Christian church, was a woman – Mary, the mother of Jesus[22].

Women serving in Jesus' ministry

Here's what we do know from the scriptures – Jesus involved both men and women in his ministry. Women, just like men, consistently played direct and significant roles serving in Jesus' ministry.

- The bible tells us that Jesus' female followers were '*many*'[23] and that they were deeply involved in the work Jesus was doing. They followed Jesus and travelled alongside him and the twelve disciples. They were counted as disciples, were taught by Jesus and allowed to take the posture of a rabbinical pupil[24] - as we see in the example of Mary of Bethany - at a time when it was viewed as only acceptable for men to be in this position. Women cared for Jesus in Galilee and Jerusalem[25], anointed him[26] and contributed from their own material resources to support Jesus' ministry[27]. Among the named women were Joanna, the wife of Herod's business manager, as well as Salome, Susanna and Mary Magdalene from whom Jesus had cast out demons. In fact Mary Magdalene was a prominent female figure in the life of Jesus and the early church – she was present at the death, burial and resurrection of Jesus and was commissioned by Christ himself on the first apostolic mission of announcing his resurrection. Her name is mentioned thirteen times in all four gospels[28], more than most of the apostles.

- Jesus also elevated women in his teachings and made them central to the deep theological truths he was teaching to his mixed-gender audience. Luke 15 records Jesus preaching a trilogy of parables to demonstrate the heart and nature of God: the parable of the lost sheep, the parable of the lost coin and the parable of the lost (prodigal) son. The second (middle) parable of the lost coin[29], puts a woman as the protagonist in the story to demonstrate God's character and heart towards his people. In the patriarchal society of the day, the telling of this female-centred narrative about God would've blown the listeners' minds (and still blows our minds today).

  Similarly, Jesus placed a woman at the centre in the parable where the kingdom of God is likened to yeast which a woman places in dough[30]. Using a parable of a persistent widow[31], Jesus taught his followers how they should persevere in prayer to God. The parable of the ten virgins[32] taught his male and female followers how they were to remain vigilant and prepare for the final coming of the bridegroom.

- Even right till the end of Jesus' life, at his crucifixion, we see women featuring prominently in the recorded scriptures. As the Roman soldiers led Jesus to the place where he would be crucified, among those following him were women, who wailed and mourned at what they were seeing. Jesus turned and addressed these women directly, giving a prophetic message of the future time to come, saying '*Daughters of Jerusalem, do not weep for me; weep for yourselves and for your children .... For if people do these things when the tree is green, what will happen when it is dry?*'[33]

  As Jesus was dying on the cross, and many who had known him had fled and gone into hiding for fear of the ramifications of being identified as a disciple and follower, we see that these faithful women[34] remained there. Among them were Mary Magdalene, Mary the mother of James and Joseph, the mother of Zebedee's sons, as well as Mary the mother of Jesus and his mother's sister, Mary the wife of Clopas, together with the disciple James. These women displayed courage and fortitude and placed themselves in the glaring, critical spotlight of onlookers, out of love and devotion to their Savior.

Jesus' elevation of women

God's purpose for us did not change. Jesus did not usher in a new dispensation, but rather was demonstrating through his actions and his teachings the unchanging heart of God and the mandate that God has always given us, male and female. This was God's mandate for us at the beginning of creation, and it is still his mandate for us today. The learned teachers and leaders of the religious institutions often found themselves in opposition to the Son of God himself. They believed that Jesus, the same who was with God at the beginning and who gave us the law, was a heretic!

Jesus' inclusive approach and redemptive mission persuasively communicated a new, powerful, alternate narrative, and showed us the way forward. Jesus exercised wisdom in how he brought about a revolutionary cultural, social and spiritual revolution. He moved from a base of some familiarity for that culture, and from this profoundly demonstrated and taught a better way, bringing about a revolutionary transformation. Jesus was deliberate and meticulous in the words he spoke and the actions he took. His counter cultural approach towards women was thus intentional, and the world was irrevocably changed as a result. Imagine those women disciples whom Jesus included in all his firsts, those who followed him during his earthly ministry and who spread the news after his resurrection – women like Mary Magdalene, Mary of Bethany, Mary the mother of Jesus, Martha and the Samaritan woman - imagine if they'd stayed silent and did not speak of what they knew. Imagine how different things would be for us as believers. Imagine how much poorer spiritually we would be today.

And thus to inform our understanding of our roles as men and women of God and the status of women in God's eyes and his kingdom, it is wise to follow the example of how Jesus interacted with and included women in his purposes.

CHAPTER 6

The Role of Women in the 1st Century Church

After Jesus' death and resurrection about 120 of his disciples who had followed Jesus in his earthly ministry were praying in the upper room - men and women who included among them 11 of the original 12 disciples, as well as Mary Magdalene, Mary the mother of Jesus and Jesus' brothers[1]. As they prayed, the Holy Spirit descended in power on the men and women alike, and they went out proclaiming the gospel to the public in various tongues, thus birthing the 1st century church just as Jesus had promised them. Imagine Mary the mother of Jesus out on those streets, powerfully proclaiming the gospel in tongues!

At Pentecost, under the power of the Holy Spirit, Peter gives one of the most brilliantly insightful public sermons on Jesus' ministry on earth, the breaking of the curse of sin and death through Jesus' death and resurrection, the promise of salvation and the revolutionary way the new ecclesia would work going forward, to bring to reality the kingdom of God.

Peter reminds the crowd of the Old Testament Joel prophecy about the last days, a period which started with the arrival of John the Baptist and Jesus' time on earth, and which we as the global body of believers are now in. The prophecy states that God will pour out his Spirit without discrimination or preference on *all* who repent and are baptized in the Holy Spirit and accept his salvation.

> 'But this is what was uttered through the prophet Joel: "*And in the last days it shall be*", God declares, "*that I will pour out my Spirit on all flesh, and your sons and your daughters shall prophesy, and your young men shall see visions, and your old men shall dream dreams; even on my male servants and female servants in those days I will pour out my Spirit, and they shall prophesy.*"'[2]

Peter goes on to encourage the crowd and for emphasis summarises the above declaration[3] again:

> 'Peter said to them, "*Repent and be baptized every one of you in the name of Jesus Christ for the forgiveness of your sins, and you will receive the gift of the Holy Spirit. For the promise is for you and for your children and for all who are far off, everyone whom the Lord our God calls to himself.*"'

In the Old Testament times, the Holy Spirit is shown to empower select Jewish people for great exploits with God. Pentecost however announces a level playing field for all in the fulfilment of the great commission and the advancement of God's kingdom mandate on earth. Race, ethnicity, background, social standing, gender, age, marital status, parental status and nationality – none of these are differentiators for the outpouring of God's grace, power, gifting and anointing among believers in these latter days. The Body of Christ is to be a community that has the indwelling of the Holy Spirit, with believers whose ministries and callings are not based on any differentiating social criteria, but are Spirit-led and Spirit empowered. This is a radical, revolutionary agenda for the ecclesia. A spiritual and social agenda that was not restricted to just tackling poverty (the poor, widows and orphans) but also righting social, structural and perceived spiritual inequality and injustice.

After Paul became a believer, in Galatians 3: 26-29 he further expounded on this egalitarian belief and this social and spiritual agenda[4]:

> *'So in Christ Jesus you are all children of God through faith, for all of you who were baptized into Christ have clothed yourselves with Christ. There is neither Jew nor Gentile, neither slave nor free, nor is there male and female, for you are all one in Christ Jesus. If you belong to Christ, then you are Abraham's seed, and heirs according to the promise.'*

There is neither Jew nor Gentile, neither slave nor free, neither male nor female in God's salvation and purpose for his ecclesia. This would've been shocking when it was publicly spoken. These three examples used here by Paul relate to structural and social inequality of power, authority and identity in the culture of the day. The inferior gentiles were not believed to have the same spiritual access rights to God as the chosen Jews. An inferior slave was owned by another human being and did not have the same social and legal rights and standing as his superior and free master. Women were not afforded the same social, legal and spiritual rights and standing as men, and were considered inferior to men.

Paul's teaching on these three social groups was a radical disruption to the status quo. God and the powerful outworking of his Holy Spirit were not reserved for the chosen or select superior few. Each of these hitherto discriminated against groups (gentiles, slaves and women) now were declared to have equal standing before God and the same authority to operate in the power of the Holy Spirit as co-heirs with Christ, for the fulfilment of the kingdom mandate. Women were declared to be part of God's restorative mandate. This spiritual and social agenda addressed the prevailing culture through the restoration of the honor, worth and social standing of half of the human population, women. A restoration of God's mandate for his female image bearers, so that the full expression of

God and his kingdom may be manifest.

Paul goes on in Galatians 3: 26-29 to expand on what this means for us as children of God - in God's kingdom we are all Abraham's seed and heirs according to the promise. Paul reinforces here also Jesus' public proclamation that female believers are daughters of Abraham. The previously understood cultural, societal and religious hierarchies, privileges and limitations are obsolete in God's kingdom. We are all called as heirs of Christ to his great commission on earth and to the power of the Holy Spirit in us. We all have a calling from God and are given spiritual gifts for the God-ordained season we are in. And that is irrevocable[5].

Women and ministry in the early church

Just as we saw how women were used by God in the Old Testament and learnt about Jesus' restorative mandate for women during his earthly ministry, so also in the 1st century church women are seen to occupy even more prominent roles in the community of believers[6].

This ecclesia that was ushered in by Jesus, and birthed through the Holy Spirit on the day of Pentecost, demonstrated its belief and commitment to this mission by accepting women in positions of leadership authority and strategic influence.

The women who followed Jesus during his earthly ministry, along with his mother Mary, were counted among the 120 male and female disciples who were praying together in the upper room[7], contrary to the Jewish tradition that would see men and women worshipping separately.

The Holy Spirit fell on the male and female disciples alike on the day of Pentecost, birthing the new 1st century church[8]. In this new church women exercised the spiritual gifts of tongues, prophecy, teaching and leadership. It included women who were apostles, deacons, evangelists, teachers and prophets[9].

The 1st century church operated with such a sense of urgency and conviction to fulfil their mission and call as God's ecclesia, that they took an all hands on deck approach engaging all disciples' full participation, men and women alike, in its mission. Before Saul became the apostle Paul, during his persecution of the new church he arrested and imprisoned men *and* women[10]. These women were not just playing private support roles or looking after the material needs of the male believers. Women played significant roles in the propagation of the gospel and the church - so much so that Saul considered them a threat and incarcerated them too. In fact, one of the reasons the early Christian message spread so quickly is because all believers, women and men, were empowered and given equal access in the evangelistic sharing of the gospel to all.

After Paul's conversion he demonstrated this commission commitment in the public letter to the Roman church[11], where he addresses the women known to be in public ministry with the same phrases he uses to refer to the men in ministry with him. Paul honors these women not in terms of their character, but in terms of their ministry, just as he does the men.

Phoebe was a deacon of the church[12] in Cenchreae and was tasked by Paul to deliver the letter of Romans to the church in Rome.

Junia[13] was a believer in the 1st century church before Paul's conversion. She was imprisoned for her faith together with Paul and others. Paul praised her as a fellow apostle and called her, together with Andronicus, 'my kinsmen'.

Tryphaena, Tryphosa, and Persis are commended by Paul as women 'who work hard in the Lord'[14], a term also used in the bible to describe Paul's own ministry[15].

In other letters to the church, Paul acknowledged Nympha[16] who held church in her house.

Chloe[17] had an influential and leading role in the church in Corinth.

Euodia and Syntyche[18] were called Paul's 'co-laborers' in Philippi, and they 'contended at Paul's side in the cause of the gospel' along with other male leaders like Clement.

The apostle John's second epistle is written to 'the lady chosen by God'[19] and acknowledges her sister, a woman also 'chosen by God'.

Tabitha (Dorkas) from Joppa and Damaris in Athens were disciples[20]. There are also honorable mentions in the scriptures of Julia, Nereus' sister, Olympus and Rufus' mother[21].

Philip the evangelist's four unmarried daughters were all prophets[22].

Lydia[23] was a church planter. She hosted the first European church, started with a group of women, in her home. Her invitation to Paul opened Galatia to the gospel.

Paul praises Timothy's grandmother Lois and his mother Eunice[24] for their faith which they imparted to Timothy, teaching him the Old Testament scriptures.

Priscilla[25] was part of the apostolic team that founded the church in Corinth and Ephesus and is commended by Paul as a 'co-worker in Christ Jesus', the same ministry phrase he uses to refer to Timothy. Paul refers to Priscilla many times in the context of ministry and mentions her in three public letters that were sent to churches across Asia. Together with her husband Aquila she was one of the church's earliest missionaries and an exemplary teacher of the gospel. She is recorded in the scriptures as correcting the teaching of Paul's fellow male apostle, Apollos.

These examples demonstrate the 1st century church's commitment to act as God's ecclesia in accordance with the Joel prophecy, and to carry on the lived example of Jesus' ministry with regards to the role women played in speaking out, not remaining silent, sharing and propagating the gospel, teaching, and exercising authority in the community of believers.

PART 3

Case Study - The Calling of Mary

CHAPTER 7

A Woman Called

The magnitude of the damage done at the Fall was so devastating that to restore it would require God himself to intervene and step into a fallen world. And God would do so through a virgin birth many generations later. So right there in the Garden of Eden, when God delivers the first messianic prophecy, is sealed the destiny and calling of a woman, Mary the mother of Jesus.

> '*And I will put enmity between you (Satan) and the woman, and between your offspring and hers; he will crush your head, and you will strike his heel.*'[1]

And it's the story of a calling far more dramatic than even Moses' experience at the burning bush or Paul's Damascus Road experience with God. Mary was to be entrusted with the revelation of a centuries old promise that God himself was coming down to earth to save humankind from the curse of sin and death. The same God who was there at the beginning, who created the world, who threw Satan from heaven, who was there at the fall of man, and in whose image we are made. The God that Mary served. That very same God would now leave his throne in heaven, transmute across space and time to become flesh and dwell amongst men. God himself would live among those he created and teach them personally through his living example, actions and words who he is, who we are in him and how we are to live. And he would come in the form of a baby boy which she, Mary, would carry, birth, protect, parent and serve.

This was HUGE.

This was earth shattering in terms of the natural laws of the universe. This was a momentous event in the history of mankind, the world and in the relationship between humans and God. And so it stands to reason that such a momentous message would take a celestial visitation by the archangel Gabriel, the messenger of God known as the angel of revelation or announcement and who '*stands in the presence of God*'[2]. An occurrence so out of this natural world that when Gabriel appears to announce the good news he says 'Do not be afraid'[3]. The appearance of this heavenly being would have been extraordinary and frightening.

In fact, consider how these history making events are carefully orchestrated by God.

First he sends Gabriel to Zechariah to announce the birth of John the Baptist, the forerunner who would '*make ready a people prepared for the (coming of the) Lord*'[4].

Then in the sixth month of Elizabeth's pregnancy, God sends Gabriel to Mary[5] to tell her that she will conceive the Lord, the Son of the Most High, who was foretold of old.

And then finally the angel of God appears to the shepherds on the day that Jesus is born[6], to announce that the Messiah, the Lord, has arrived on earth!

When that final birth announcement was complete '*a great company of the heavenly host appeared with the angel of God, praising God and saying, "Glory to God in the highest heaven, and on earth peace to those on whom his favor rests*[7].'" This gave those shepherds, and those of us reading this recorded scripture today, a glimpse of what Revelation also reveals about the heavenly realm - where legions of angels are in worship of God day and night[8]. Those legions of angels were acutely watching as God orchestrated this chain of events as the Son, who is with the Father and was with him from the beginning, is incarnated on earth to live amongst men.

If we honestly reflect on this we would realise that we largely tend to underestimate or under-imagine the scale of what God did here and what was going on in the heavenly realm when the virgin Mary was approached by the angel.

You see, those very same angels also bore witness to the fall of Satan from heaven[9], taking a third of the angels with him. They were witnesses to the creation of the world and human beings, and to the fall of man. They were witness to the first messianic prophecy by God himself in the Garden of Eden. And the time had now come for the foretold redemption of the world by God himself.

And if there is rejoicing in heaven when one sinner repents[10], you bet that when the time arrived for that messianic prophecy to be realised on earth, to redeem the world from sin, all of heaven was watching. And when the day finally came and God was incarnated on earth, the heavenly hosts rejoiced mightily!

This was HUGE.

And amid this momentous turn of history, a betrothed young woman called Mary receives her calling.

CHAPTER 8

Highly Favored

In the case of Mary, we are told that it is the archangel Gabriel who announces to Mary the coming of God to earth. In the Old and New Testaments we find records of other supernatural visitations[1] either by an angel of the Lord (to Hagar, Samson's mother and Zechariah) or by God himself (to Abram) that relate to announcements about the births and destinies of major biblical characters such as Ishmael, Samson, John the Baptist and Isaac.

Mary was an ordinary young woman. In fact, so ordinary was she that there is no biblical record of her family background or social standing. An ordinary young woman who was visited by a powerful angel who had been sent by an extraordinary God.

To say that Gabriel's visitation caught Mary by surprise is an understatement. So when the angel Gabriel addresses Mary as highly favored[2] by God, Mary was greatly troubled, stunned into silence by his words, and she wondered what kind of greeting this might be.

Mary was let in on the Godly secret that the long-foretold Messiah was now coming to earth and given the news that she would be responsible for birthing and raising the Son of God. God selected this young woman from a small, insignificant town outside of Galilee.

This was not news she (or Joseph) was expecting.

Mary and Joseph may not have known it, but God knew right from the fall in the Garden of Eden the exact time and point in history he would come down to earth and to whom the announcement would be made. God is not a random, accidental kind of God. He is purposeful, deliberate. He knew exactly the steps that he would take and whom he would call.

An obedient servant

As Mary remained silent, Gabriel continued to tell Mary that she would conceive a son, called Jesus. Upon hearing Gabriel's message, Mary responded, '*How can this be?*' Unlike Zechariah a few months earlier[3], Mary did not respond out of unbelief. Yes, this is a future she had not planned or foreseen, but Mary asked this question because she was a virgin and had not had sex with a man, and was not sure how she was to become pregnant.

Here we have the first indication of the type of woman Mary was and her level of faith. The circumstances in her life did not result in her first reaction being one of unbelief or dismissal but rather curiosity about how God would accomplish this.

Gabriel informed Mary that she would conceive not through natural means, but through the Holy Spirit.

Gabriel informed Mary that she *would* conceive. She was not yet pregnant. God announced his *intention* to Mary. God is not a God who forces his will on us. He chooses us, but it is our choice to surrender to His will and to walk in our calling. So in theory, Mary had a choice to refuse to surrender to the calling God had placed on her life. She could have decided the price was too high to pay. She could have objected to the news because this was not what she and Joseph, two righteous, God-fearing and faithful servants of God, had planned. She could've rejected the idea because she had no idea what the future held, how this could turn out, how this could be done. She could've succumbed to fear or unbelief. As she was alone when the angel appeared to her, and there were no other witnesses, she could've walked away and doubted if she had even truly seen what she'd seen or heard what she'd heard. She could've started to think that it was a figment of her imagination, or her own human flights of fancy.

When God comes with something that seems implausible or impossible, we can all be tempted to take one of these routes. In trying to make sense of it, we can grapple with the battle of our thoughts, logic and will. And some of us can run from our calling for a long time, as Jonah did. Often simply because it does not make sense, or we fear the price we will have to pay.

But we see that Mary made a choice to surrender to God, to trust his perfect will, to obey him and to walk in her calling: '*I am the Lord's servant, may your word to me be fulfilled*[4].' Mary exercised obedience not to a man, a society, a culture or even a religion, but full obedience to God her maker. For Mary this was a highly disruptive and risky, even dangerous, story to her life. Mary shows here incredible spiritual maturity and faith in an almighty God in the face of an unknown future and potential social isolation and ostracism. She understood that a life of faith was not about desiring an almighty God to fulfil the plans we have for our lives, but rather we are to be obedient to God's will and serve God in his plan for our lives, whatever that may require of us.

God chooses us for his work not because we are strong enough or smart enough or recognised by others as being important or capable. He chooses us and asks us to be willing to trust him and follow him, as he does what only he can do.

Prophecy

There were of course prophecies that foretold some of Mary's destiny and calling, not least of which was the first messianic prophecy by God himself at the Fall in the Garden of Eden[5], foretelling how the woman's offspring would crush Satan's head. The Old Testament prophets too foretold that a virgin would conceive[6] and give birth to the Messiah, and he will come from out of Bethlehem from the line of David - circumstances which matched those of Mary's life. And of course there was also the divine word of knowledge uttered by a pregnant Elizabeth to Mary upon their meeting:

> '*Blessed are you among women, and blessed is the child you will bear! But why am I so favored, that the mother of my Lord should come to me? As soon as the sound of your greeting reached my ears, the baby in my womb leaped for joy. Blessed is she who has believed that the Lord would fulfill his promises to her!*'[7]

This supernatural confirmation of the promise of God uttered by Elizabeth, prompted Mary to sing a spontaneous song of praise to God. When Mary had delivered the baby Jesus, the supernaturally guided visits from the Magi[8] and the shepherds[9] again brought more confirmation about the destiny of the child Jesus and the calling of Mary. Forty days after Jesus' birth Mary and Joseph brought him to the temple in Jerusalem to complete Mary's ritual purification after childbirth, and to consecrate Jesus as the firstborn son in accordance to Jewish custom[10]. Simeon's prophecy to Mary in particular, as they enter the temple, foretold the destiny of the child and also the cost and pain Mary would experience in the realization of that calling. In addition, the prophet Anna also meets the family at the temple entrance and further confirms the divine nature and destiny of the child Jesus.

During that season of her calling in which she was raising the young Jesus, Mary is said to have kept to herself all these incredible things that were happening and pondered on them in her heart[11].

CHAPTER 9

A Woman's Mandate

It bears to reason that with such a momentous moment in history God would be sure to execute it in such a way that would send a clear message to all about his character, and how he chooses to work and operate. Right? God is not random. He is meticulous. He is intentional. He is purposeful.

To announce the coming birth of a first born male, and the incarnation of the promised Messiah at that, it could be thought to be culturally appropriate for the angel to bring such knowledge and revelation to the fiancé who would be deemed the patriarch and head in the new family. But the angel made his announcement not to Mary's father, her soon-to-be husband, the high priest, a male prophet or to the ruler of the synagogue, but rather to just Mary herself, on her own. And then later to Elizabeth, Mary's cousin.

This was a young, betrothed woman, in a culture where women had few social rights and were vulnerable outside of the covering of a male. Her partner Joseph would be expected to exercise headship over her in marriage, as understood in the Jewish religious and cultural norms of the time. He was a descendant in the line of David. As a Jewish man this son would be considered by society as his first born, the legal male heir to his name and legacy. And yet God chose not to include Joseph in the beginning of this story.

By the time the angel appeared to Joseph, we are told that the plan of God and the calling on Mary's life had already commenced – she had already conceived. Joseph had not received advance first hand notification of God's plan. Not sure what to make of the situation, he'd decided that he was going to divorce Mary. The poor man initially had no clue what was going on. While Mary was informed of God's intention, Joseph did not have a choice in the matter. It was already done. Mary was pregnant.

So why would God speak to Mary on her own about the long foretold Jewish prophecy that is about to be fulfilled, knowing the burden it would place on her to explain herself to her betrothed and to her family? We can assume that this would've been a very strained and difficult conversation for all to have. The understandable confusion, misunderstanding and suspicion that would bring. The shame, ostracism, gossip and humiliation that could possibly bring. The potential termination of a marriage of two righteous and innocent people. Mary may possibly have had to walk out her calling as a single woman in a society where she would've been vulnerable. Why would God not send the angel to speak to both her and Joseph when they are either together or at least inform them at the same time, even if separately, and before conception?

And neither can this be explained away by the idea that it is because Mary would be the one to bear and nurse this child. The angel similarly appeared to the priest Zechariah to announce that he and his apparently barren wife Elizabeth would have a child - John the Baptist, the one who would pave the way for Christ's ministry on earth[1].

God's challenge to us all when we get the call is this: that we are not to rely just on the words or the circumstances we think we humanly understand. We should also ponder and reflect on God's actions. Watch what God does with and through people and thus understand who he is and what that says about who we are in him. This goes beyond the cultural, social and religious paradigms of our understanding. This goes beyond academic expounding. This is about a God who understands the universe and the intention for his creation so much better than we ever could. His actions speaks so much louder. Jesus did this very thing so well during his earthly lifetime - his actions spoke so much louder than those who studied and taught the law and scriptures could encapsulate, explain or understand.

If at his historic coming to earth God was going to send a clear message here for all of his followers henceforth about what he is about and how he views us, then we better look closely at what he does and how he does it. God deliberately and purposefully chose to bring this most incredible revelation to Mary alone. One of the biggest, most important things that would happen since the creation of humankind. Why? Because this was the story of her calling, this engaged young woman, Mary. And the way God chooses to announce the start of that calling points to a mandate that goes beyond a mothering role in the natural – it is that of a disciple who would go on to champion the kingdom long after the death of Christ. Mary's key role in God's redemption story is referenced in the record of Jesus' genealogy, where Joseph is referred to as '*the husband of Mary*'[2] (as opposed to Joseph whose wife was Mary, or Joseph who was married to Mary).

We should not conflate our own understanding of headship in a marital relationship with how God would choose to exercise calling in and for the kingdom. When we answer intellectually, we say yes of course not. But if we examine the historic sociocultural evidence, we realise that we have by extension done exactly that. Churches, and the teaching and internal culture within churches, have frequently acted as gatekeepers regarding the extent to which Christian wives may exercise their God-ordained gifting and calling and may rise (become visible) in relation to their husbands.

We see demonstrated here in Mary's story that God is the one who chooses and calls out. God's deliberate choice of actions demonstrate again that with God there is no preferential standing. Men and women of all backgrounds are equally able to come face to face with the calling of God on their lives, and that God calls all according to his will, even women in marital relationships.

CHAPTER 10

Partnership in Marriage

This exploration of Mary's calling does not suggest though that Joseph was not a worthy, righteous man – indeed he was. We are told in the scriptures that he was '*faithful to the law*'[1] and we see also from his later actions that he was a man of upright character and deep spiritual faith and discernment (he recognised God's guidance in his dreams and obeyed).

Neither does it suggest that Joseph did not have a pivotal role to play. Though Mary receives this call, Joseph too is called to protect this promise of the Messiah. There were many instances as they walk out this calling together, that this couple experience lack of clarity, uncertainty, changes and disruptions, and times where Joseph alone, not Mary, received knowledge and instruction from God of what next step to take.

Joseph a suitable partner to Mary

God invites Joseph to partner with Mary in this calling[2]. Joseph obeys this direction and marries Mary, thus providing her with the social protections she needed as a woman in that society. Throughout the unfolding of this calling, we continue to see Joseph's commitment to his responsibility and to God's instructions, so that God's purposes are fulfilled. He abstains from being intimate with Mary[3] until after Jesus' birth. Following Jesus' birth in Bethlehem, Joseph is told by an angel in a dream to take the family to Egypt to escape Herod's planned massacre of the children of Bethlehem[4]. He provides for the family through his work as a carpenter[5]. Joseph, together with Mary, also takes the infant Jesus to the temple to be blessed, as per Jewish custom[6] – it is here that they both receive further prophetic confirmation from both Simeon and Anna of Jesus' mission.

Joseph was a very suitable partner for Mary in this calling.

They needed each other to fulfil their destinies. God required both Mary and Joseph to hear, obey and act in unison and in partnership to support the fulfilment of the calling given. Partners in the mandate. Joseph was from the line of David[7], and thus Jesus' legal lineage comes through Joseph. Joseph was given dreams to protect and safeguard God's promise in Mary and the life of the young Jesus. Mary was required to trust the direction given to Joseph by God, to support that promise which was given to her. Their empowering partnership was one of mutual submission, love, honor, collaboration, other-centredness and shared purpose.

In the 1st century women's standing in society or in the home was inferior to men, and marriage brought women under the household of the man in a subservient status. A woman did not have the right to divorce her husband. A husband could however divorce his wife for any reason he saw fit.

And yet here we see modelled for us God's intention for a relationship of mutuality so that men and women can walk out their calling in harmony, reflecting the fullness of God's image. Joseph models mutual submission to the suitable partner God had given him, just as Mary models this with Joseph. Both are committed to obeying God's agenda first and foremost, above any cultural understanding of their gender roles or privileges. And together they model a dynamic that the 1st century church and we today are instructed to follow.

Mutual submission in Jesus' ecclesia

As believers we are taught in the bible that in our relationships and interactions with others we are to submit to one another, humble ourselves for the benefit of others and to count others as more significant than ourselves[8]. This is relevant for all believers, both single and married. These bible passages do not exclude these requirements for the marital relationship between two believers.

In Ephesians 5: 22-30 we are told what this mutual submission of believers looks like in the context of marriage. Husbands are instructed to give themselves to their wives as Christ the Savior gave himself to the church, and to love their wives as much as they love their own bodies. Paul's instructions to husbands here, within the context of the society of that day and the inferior position of women in it, would have been astounding. And in a dynamic of mutual submission and love, wives are to give honor to their husbands as to Christ himself. This text about submission does not reflect an interpretation of authoritative dominance of the husband over his wife (neither does it condone domination of the wife over the husband). Out of love Christ our Savior died for us, and through his death redeemed us, his bride. That is the selfless, sacrificial standard referred to here.

As we've read, Jesus afforded women the same dignity and respect as men when he interacted with them. In the 1st century society where divorce was a male privilege, and women were regarded as the husband's property, Jesus was challenged by teachers of the law about the circumstances under which a man may divorce his wife[9]. Jesus answered instead,

> "*Haven't you read, that at the beginning the Creator 'made them male and female' and said, 'For this reason a man will leave his father and mother and be united to his wife, and the two will become one flesh'. So they are no*

longer two, but one flesh. Therefore what God has joined together, let no one separate."

What a reversal of the societal understanding of the power dynamics in a marital relationship between a husband and wife! The two become *one*. The emphasis here is not placed on a societal contract that brings the woman into and under submission of the man and his household, but rather that two people come together as one, in one union and purpose under God. Two image bearers together reflecting one God. And what God puts together, let no man separate – a challenge if ever there was one, to the pervasive cultural understanding of the society. In intentionally referencing the scriptures from man and woman's pre-Fall state of being in Genesis[10], Jesus here gives his approval to a mutually honoring marital relationship where women are vested under God with the same status and dignity as their male spouse.

This is a radical and restorative approach for society - that which is modelled at home will be emulated in the society at large. It is a social agenda that displays the kingdom of God, where the value and dignity of all human beings is evident in the way society conducts and structures itself, even in the home. The kingdom of God that is like salt and light which transforms the fabric of the home, and spreads from the home transforming the fabric of society. An ecclesia birthed in and emanating from the homes of righteous believers in unity of purpose.

If this dynamic of mutuality was not the original intention of God's creation, and of Jesus' teachings and lived example, the many stories of women intentionally and deliberately included in the scriptures by male authors would be considered an abomination. Stories of married women like Deborah, Abigail and Sarah. Deborah rose to national civic and spiritual leadership, advising an all-male army to lead a nation towards victory and the promise God had for Israel[11]. And yet nothing is known of her husband or his activity, except his name. God himself tells Abraham to submit to his wife Sarah's plan[12]. Abigail, who in her actions is distinctively unsubmissive to her husband Nabal's actions and approach, is portrayed in the bible as a woman of wisdom, and because of her actions she is shown favor by David[13]. In contrast, her husband is struck dead by God.

Like Mary and Joseph, Priscilla and Aquila are another committed, married couple who operated in unison and who are positively mentioned in the bible. In the scriptures their names always appear together, not individually. They both worked together as tentmakers, learnt and taught the gospel together, held church in their home, travelled with Paul as ministry partners, and remained close friends with Paul right up until his death[14]. Their lives were centred on Christ and their commitment to the advancement of God's kingdom. There is no emphasis given in the scriptures to Priscilla's roles as mother and wife – in fact we do not even know if they had any children. Priscilla's actions in the propagation and teaching of the gospel, in partnership with her husband, are a portrait of strong purpose-centred womanhood.

These examples are highlighted here, not to make a point of any preference for one gender over another or as examples of women who did better. Rather these examples demonstrate that God chooses whom he wills and has always desired for men and women to fulfil the dominion mandate and walk out their calling in him together. Mary, Priscilla and Deborah were each very different married women with very different callings. For example, Mary did not have a formal occupation like Priscilla (tent making business) or Deborah (national leader) did. Their stories show that there's no standard, one-size-fits-all, homogenous way in which Christians are to conduct a synergistic marital partnership on a day-to-day basis. What their stories have in common is that they had mutually honoring and supportive dynamics within their marriages that fortified the specific unique callings they faced.

These couples prioritised fulfilling God's commands and his will above all other understanding of their gender or societal roles, privileges or expectations.

For married Christians a strong, healthy and mutually empowering marriage is a solid foundation for effectively walking out their calling. Sadly, many Christian marriages have been held back from reaching their full potential because of an unbalanced understanding of male 'headship'. Equal value, common purpose and mutuality was founded in creation and God has never deviated from this. These stories challenge us to similar discipleship.

CHAPTER 11

A Woman of Substance

Just like we often under-imagine the coming of Christ to earth, as we discussed previously, so also we often underestimate the story of Mary. If we truly reflect on it, Mary's story is often reduced that of a naïve young woman to whom the incarnation of Christ happened and whose sole responsibility was to do the dutiful womanly thing - to carry this child in pregnancy and mother the child during its formative years. But Mary was so much more than a mother, and neither was she just a naïve person who fell into a parenting role.

When we read the joyful praise song Mary sang when she met with Elizabeth, we see that Mary (like Elizabeth) had a clear and insightful understanding of what God was doing in all of this. The hymn, Mary's Magnificat, is found in Luke 1: 46-55:

46 *And Mary said:*

"*My soul glorifies the Lord*
47 *and my spirit rejoices in God my Savior,*
48 *for he has been mindful*
of the humble state of his servant.
From now on all generations will call me blessed,
49 *for the Mighty One has done great things for me —*
holy is his name.
50 *His mercy extends to those who fear him,*
from generation to generation.
51 *He has performed mighty deeds with his arm;*
he has scattered those who are proud in their inmost thoughts.

52 *He has brought down rulers from their thrones*
but has lifted up the humble.
53 *He has filled the hungry with good things*
but has sent the rich away empty.
54 *He has helped his servant Israel,*
remembering to be merciful
55 *to Abraham and his descendants forever,*
just as he promised our ancestors."

Mary was a woman who knew God's word

Mary's song is filled with phrase after phrase of scripture. The words of the her song allude to phrases in Psalm 13, Psalm 22, Psalm 25, Psalm 44, Psalm 89, Psalm 98, and Psalm 147. She also alludes to Hannah's prayer in 1 Samuel 2: 2-10 when God granted her a child. Mary delved into the breadth of the known scriptures to formulate the words of her praise to God for the amazing thing he had done for her by calling her into his messianic plan, and what he will do also for all of those who are called his own.

And when we see this, we understand how a young woman could have shown such maturity of faith in the face of the surprise announcement by Gabriel. Mary understood very well the potential dangers of her calling: societal ostracism, possible loss of her husband Joseph, being cut off from her family and other personal and physical dangers. But because of her knowledge of the scriptures that informed her faith, she did not respond in unbelief. She believed and surrendered to God's will. And it's that same scriptural knowledge we see here in the song she sings.

Mary is an example to us. Just like Mary, we too need to grow in our knowledge and understanding of the scriptures to grow our faith, recognise and grasp the sovereignty of God and the calling he has on our lives, and to run the race set out before us.

Mary was a woman who knew her God

Mary understood God's multi-generational way of working and knew her people's history with God. She was acquainted with all the many ways God had throughout history dealt with his chosen people, and also those who oppose God's will and God's people. Here was a woman who may have been vulnerable and faced isolation, yet she expressed confidence in a righteous God whom she knew was sovereign and mighty. The same God who had accomplished these things in the past was on her side.

She also knew the covenant God had with his people. She knew that since that Genesis 3:15 messianic prophecy, God had been working on his redemptive plan for the world through the promised Christ, the Messiah. She knew the promises of God spoken to Abraham, Isaac, Jacob, Moses, David and Jeremiah. She knew what Jesus would accomplish for his people and for the advancement of God's kingdom. She had meditated on these promises of God and knew what she could confidently expect from him. She understood the importance and significance of the moment - that God would fulfil his promises. We also see later evidence of her knowledge of his deity and power, when she asks him to perform the first miracle and he turns water into wine at the wedding in Cana[1].

Mary also understood God's way of working – a subversive, radical way that is contrary to human inclination – '*He lifts up the humble and fills the hungry with good things while sending the rich away empty.*' Oh yes, she knew this subversive, radical Jesus she was carrying and what he had come to do on this earth!

Mary was a woman of great character and humility

Since the Garden of Eden and the promise given to Abraham[2], the Israelites had been waiting for that seed that would crush the head of the serpent. And now Mary bore the knowledge given to her by the angel Gabriel, and confirmed again by the word of knowledge from Elizabeth, that she had been given an incredibly honorable and influential task. Her calling and her life purpose had been revealed to her. She was the Messiah-bearer.

And her response was one of humility. This woman, who was going to play a significant role in bringing the Savior into this world, acknowledged that she was a sinner and needed a Savior. She also stated that she was of humble position and a servant of the Lord. This was a woman of character who understood servanthood and did not become proud or seduced by the biblical or historical significance of her position or calling.

And despite the challenges of her circumstances, Mary's song is filled with thankfulness. She was an unwed pregnant woman facing a possibly dangerous and difficult life ahead. At the time it would've been half a millennium since the Israelites had a king on the throne and the Romans were occupying the land. And who knows the full reason for her 3-month stay with Elizabeth, and where her family were in all of this, during a time when she needed immense support. And yet in this song, Mary had an attitude of gratitude and hope.

By the mature understanding of God and his promises evident in Mary's song, we see that she had a heart after God. A devout believer who knew how to hear God. Mary understood the significance and the magnitude of the calling she had received. However, the focus was never on her. The focus was on Christ. For Mary it was always about God, Jesus Christ, and the kingdom purpose. This is a woman of substance.

Mary was so much more than a mother

In Luke 11: 27-28 we read about what appears initially to be a strange inclusion of a random remark regarding Jesus' mother, but which we soon get to understand would've been an exchange so jarring and profound to the people's understanding at the time, that the biblical authors make a point of recording this in the scriptures.

Jesus was teaching deep biblical truths to the crowds, and the crowds were growing in size as they listened to his wisdom and the astounding things he was saying. As he was teaching, a woman in the crowd interrupted him calling out, '*Blessed is the mother who gave you birth and nursed you.*' This was considered a high compliment and honor indeed by that society. This mother who raised such a son, that was teaching these astounding things!

However, listen to Jesus' response in verse 28 - Jesus replied, '*Blessed rather are those who hear the word of God and obey.*'

Blessed *rather* ...

Jesus' reply, in full hearing of the entire crowd of men and women alike, absolutely deflects this woman's compliment and raises the stakes by affirming the vital identity and powerful role of a woman that goes beyond the traditional motherly or marital role. Jesus calls out to the even higher honor of women and all believers and disciples like his mother, Mary. His answer alludes instead to the true gravity of the intentional, eyes-wide-open choices and counter-cultural actions Mary took when she accepted God's invitation to birth the Messiah, even though that could mean a single life of social isolation, exclusion and hardship. Jesus, being God, also knew what was ahead and what was to come for this woman.

Mary's obedience cost her much. She endured the pain and danger of giving birth in a humble stable, fleeing the murderous intentions of King Herod. She witnessed the humiliating crucifixion and excruciating death of her son and Savior as she stood weeping at the foot of the cross, when almost all of Jesus' followers hid for fear of being publicly associated with him. After Jesus' death, that same Mary was among the 120 disciples who regularly prayed together in the upper room while facing persecution, who received the Holy Spirit on the day of Pentecost, and who risked their lives in the birthing of the Christian church.

This was not the naïve woman we may be prone to believe, who just fell into a parenting role. She was neither a passive witness nor a bystander to the commission on earth. She didn't just settle for a good enough Christian walk, doing a good job of raising the Son of God. No, she hungered and thirsted for much more in her walk with her Savior. This was in fact a formidable and courageous disciple of God. A woman steadfastly walking a very radical life journey of obedience with her God. This was a woman who knew not only that the Messiah had come, but that God's kingdom had come, and that she had a role to play in that.

Mary played an important role in the miraculous fulfilment of God's purposes. Apart from the early years of Jesus' life up until Jesus was 12 years old, Mary's husband Joseph is not really mentioned again in the Bible. We do not know what happened to him. We do know however that Mary was the only human being who was present at Jesus' birth and death on earth, and at the birth of the Christian church. She was a witness to it all - a privilege she was afforded for her obedience in taking up her call.

I'm not suggesting that playing a role primarily in the home as a mother for a season or for a lifetime is not biblical for women - parenthood is an incredible human privilege for men and women, and is a part of our earthly calling which has multi-generational impact (as we discussed in Chapter 1). Neither am I suggesting that Jesus did not value motherhood and the role of mothers – the bible contains scriptures that use the nature and activities of mothers to demonstrate God's heart and character[3], as well as many other scriptures that honor the role and impact of mothers[4]. But rather, by his response Jesus was saying that she was so much more than the constraints of the prescribed primary role for women in that society and culture. That women are not only considered great when they give birth to someone great.

The childbearing years can limit the time and energy for what one can accomplish outside of the mothering role, especially as most women carry the greater burden for household activities, child care and other family care duties, and perhaps also in addition to formal employment outside of the home.

However, hear this: Raising, feeding and providing for your children is not the total extent of your calling and identity as a woman in this lifetime. Rather, blessed is the one who hears the words God speaks to them and obeys, even if it costs them. It is most important that you can attest to the fact that you are doing what God has asked of you.

You are so much more than a mother! As a co-laborer with Christ, you have in your hand the destiny of your family and of a nation, and the fulfilment of God's promises and the coming of his kingdom on earth.

PART 4

The Call to Women and the Church Today

CHAPTER 12

Women and their Calling in the Church

Throughout the scriptures we find a roll call of giants of the faith on whose shoulders we as Christian women stand today. As we contemplate their lives and testimonies, including the story of Mary, we in the contemporary church are challenged to consider the story we are going to co-create with God during our lifetime.

We've discussed how the gospel spread rapidly in the 1st century church as men and women ministered under the power of the Holy Spirit, exercising the spiritual gifts like tongues, prophecy, teaching, leadership, performing miracles and healings.

The New Testament scriptures tell us of several such gifts of the Spirit[1], some of which are listed below:

- Apostleship
- Prophecy
- Teaching
- Miracles / Healing
- Service/Helps
- Administration
- Tongues
- Leadership
- Knowledge
- Wisdom
- Discernment
- Exhortation
- Shepherding
- Faith
- Evangelism
- Mercy
- Giving
- Hospitality

The exercise of spiritual gifts by women

Peter reminded believers on the day of Pentecost that God pours out his Spirit on *all* flesh[2]. He interpreted this indiscriminate outpouring of the Spirit in light of the Joel prophecy, telling believers that God pours out his Spirit as he chooses[3] and on whom he chooses. Similarly, when Paul instructs the church on the use of the spiritual gifts, he encourages male and female believers alike to eagerly desire and use the gifts of the Spirit for the edification and building up of the church[4].

However, the exercise of the gifts of teaching and leadership by women in the church has traditionally, and still today, been fraught with challenge, largely due to the appropriation of Paul's words found in 1 Timothy 2: 11-12:

> '*A woman should learn in quietness and full submission. I do not permit a woman to teach or to assume authority over a man; she must be quiet.*'

Proponents of the prohibition of women teachers or leaders in the church justify their stance with the above text. These and other similar texts in the scriptures[5] have challenged the church in its desire to serve God truthfully, faithfully and fervently, due to the tension and seeming incompatibility which exists between these disputed texts and the texts and examples found across the entirety of the biblical scriptures. They can arguably be considered to be some of the least understood and most contested passages in scripture[6].

If we believe that we are *all* called by God for his purpose[7], that God is the one who pours out his spiritual gifts as he chooses and on whom he chooses, and that we *all* are to use these gifts to build up the church, then it's challenging to also simultaneously believe that women should not operate in the full expression of their gifts and should limit the exercise of their gifts. These beliefs are not compatible and cannot be embraced simultaneously.

In this regard the adoption of 1 Timothy 2: 11-12 as a universal biblical restriction for all women in the global church proves challenging, as it contradicts much of the rest of the bible, including Paul's own writings (e.g., on spiritual gifts and speaking prophecy). It also clearly stands in contrast to the many positively recorded examples and actions of female teachers and leaders deliberately included throughout the scriptures, and also Paul's own actions in partnering with and affirming female teachers and leaders.

Teaching in the hierarchy of spiritual gifts

Several women in the scriptures played leading roles as prophets - a reminder to the church that we are to value women's voices just as God does. These women certainly did not remain silent, and we are the beneficiaries today of their fearless acts of faith in this manner. Joel's prophecy, and Peter's confirmation of this, states that '*your sons and your daughters shall prophesy*'[8]. Paul in fact encourages *all* believers who have the gift of prophecy to use it - just as *anyone* who has the gift of teaching should teach, and *anyone* who has the gift to lead should do so diligently[9]. And today indeed we see such spiritual gifting in both men and women, in believers in the church pews as well as those leading out front on the stage.

This declaration of women and men's equivalent roles as God's instruments and mouthpieces in the new church movement is not something that can be dismissed. Neither is it correct to propose that this cross gender gift of prophecy does not equate to similar spiritual authority as teaching. Paul gives a hierarchy of the spiritual gifts[10], encouraging *all* believers to desire these *greater gifts:*

'And in the church God has appointed first of all apostles, second prophets, third teachers, then workers of miracles, and those with gifts of healing, helping, administration, and various tongues.'

Paul in fact ranks prophecy as a higher authoritative spiritual gift than teaching. By virtue of Paul's own teaching here, it doesn't seem logical to believe that a woman's gift of prophecy in the church, which Paul encourages, does not come with the equivalent spiritual authority as that of a male exercising the gift of teaching. In addition, prophecy requires speaking and includes a teaching component[11], so this too stands in contradiction to 1 Timothy 2: 11-12.

Paul's own affirmation of female teachers and leaders

As we've previously explored in Chapter 6, Paul himself positively affirmed the female teachers and leaders of the 1st century church on many occasions, in contradiction to 1 Timothy 2: 11-12. In this regard especially, the teaching incident[12] in Acts 18: 24–28 involving the church leader Priscilla warrants closer consideration. In the scriptures, Priscilla is recorded as a positive example of an adult Christian woman teaching doctrine to an adult Christian male, the apostle Apollos - a leading evangelist of the 1st century church and a friend of Paul.

As a means of putting the incident in context, the preceding verses in Acts 18: 24-25 state Apollos' credentials - we are told that he '*was a learned man, with a thorough knowledge of the Scriptures. He had been instructed in the way of the Lord, and he spoke with great fervour*'. We are also told that Apollos only knew about the baptism of John the Baptist, but did not know of the baptism taught by Jesus. Upon hearing Apollos preach, Priscilla and her husband Aquila invited him to their home to teach him this significant doctrinal distinction and '*explain to him the way of God more accurately*'.

In the recording of this teaching encounter, Priscilla's name is recorded before that of Aquila, making it challenging to conclude that she was just a bystander while her husband did the teaching, or that she did the teaching only under the covering of her husband. In fact, Priscilla's name is mentioned before that of her husband in 4 out of the 6 times[13] they are mentioned across four books in the bible, when most references to husbands and wives in the Bible usually place the man first.

Just like the testimony of Deborah, the story of Priscilla would be viewed as an abomination against an espoused belief that prohibits females to teach or lead, and viewed as usurping male authority. However, both testimonies are recorded in the scriptures as positive examples of believers moving and operating under the leading, authority and guidance of God's Spirit. Importantly, Paul himself publicly positively affirms Priscilla, together with her husband, and remains close to these fellow workers in Christ after this event and right till the end when he mentions them in the final letter he wrote shortly before his death[14].

Selective application of prohibitions and requirements

In addition to the prohibitions on teaching and exercising authority included in 1 Timothy 2: 11-12, other prohibitions on women are included in the preceding and following verses of these very same scriptures[15]: women are not permitted to worship with uncovered heads, cut their hair and wear short hairstyles, adorn themselves with '*elaborate hairstyles or gold or pearls or expensive clothes*', and are not permitted to speak in church at all. 1 Timothy 2: 15 also states that women will be saved through childbearing. These listed prohibitions and requirements are not enforced globally in the wider church today, and we certainly do not believe women are saved through childbearing.

We also see in the contemporary church that women aren't actually excluded from teaching or exercising authority and leadership over men overall. They do indeed teach and lead over males as missionaries, evangelists, in bible study groups, in home church groups, at Christian conferences, in youth and children's groups, and at weekday church events - all of which are roles and functions that play a critical role in the spiritual development of these believers, and require the exercise of spiritual authority and considerable teaching discernment, ability and gifting. Approximately 32% of UK church attendees today are single[16] (never married, divorced or widowed) - many single female missionaries, especially those stationed in remote regions, have evangelised, taught and exercised authority over males without any covering of a husband or another male.

The contemporary church appears to employ selective application of prohibitions and requirements. The drawing of such somewhat random boundary lines of where and when a woman may teach, exercise authority and disciple fellow believers thus becomes arbitrary and subjective. And as history would attest, these practices and boundaries too have changed down the centuries as culture and understanding has shifted.

So in the organised church structure there isn't therefore a blanket adherence to Paul's words in 1 Timothy 2: 11-12, with a blanket ban on women leading and teaching men. Rather, women are largely restricted from doing do so in positions of raised power, influence and visibility, such as in senior leadership teams and in frontline roles at Sunday services.

Women's exclusion from leading positions

What are we then to believe is the reason for women's exclusion from these positions of seniority and raised visibility? Are we saying that women lack spiritual gifting or anointing in these areas of teaching and leadership? Nowhere in Paul's teaching about spiritual gifts does he indicate that certain gifts are the sole remit of a particular gender. When he admonishes believers with the gift of teaching to teach, and those gifted in leadership to lead[17], he does not qualify these verses by instructing this only to men or that women with this gift should only use it in female only contexts for building up of the female half of the church body. Nor does he state that women should limit their desire for spiritual gifting to a select few gifts, and eliminate from their list the gifts of teaching or leadership. In other words, there are no spiritual gifts that are male-specific or female-specific. Paul in fact encourages male *and* female believers to support each other in discovering and exercising their spiritual gifts[18], and to use the gifts to serve others.

Or are we to say that women may receive these gifts but are not permitted to exercise them as fully or as powerfully as men? Are we therefore to say that even if women are gifted, they may not exercise their giftings and calling in positions of significance? Because that is the picture that seemingly emerges from such arguments prohibiting women from teaching and leading cross-gender groups elsewhere but not in these particular positions in the corporate church structure.

God has deliberately created diversity in all of us for his purpose and for the unique calling we receive directly from him. Men are not a homogenous group equally gifted in leadership, teaching or preaching with which they are inherently able to exercise authority and lead others. And so also, neither are women a homogenous group possessing whatever quality one may wish to suggest makes them uniquely suitable only for secondary, support roles.

And what about the Christian woman who, in exercising her God-given gifting and talents, is occupying a senior leadership position such as a CEO of a company and oversees male and female employees, with line management authority, mentorship, training and professional development responsibility and with spiritual influence over them, some of whom may actually include Christian males. This woman is walking in her unique calling as God's ecclesia within the marketplace. Is she thus acting in an unbiblical way?

Jesus' example and teachings

If despite all the contrary evidence in the entirety of the scriptures, including the actions and other teachings of Paul himself, one is to choose a dogged adherence to the prohibition of women teaching and leading in the church, and continue to dodge the dilemma of selective scriptural adherence to these prohibitions, are we thus to take the stance that Paul's teaching in these particular verses is superior and overrides the understanding we gain from the actions and teachings of Jesus himself? As we've illustrated earlier in this book, while being mindful of the prevalent cultural norms of that 1st century society, Jesus nevertheless intentionally included women and promoted the equal standing of women and men before him and in the kingdom mandate.

If we are to choose the stance that elders and leaders in the church today should only be male as Jesus chose males as the initial 12 disciples, 11 of whom became apostles in the new 1st century church leadership, should we thus also exclude from leadership any men who are not Jewish since the 12 disciples and the elders of the 1st century church were Jews. Also, we should then also adopt the requirements for church leaders and elders listed in 1 Timothy 3: 1-7 and Titus 1: 6-9, and exclude men who are recent converts, are single, have remarried after being widowed or divorced, are married but do not have children, or have children who are unbelievers or rebellious.

We know of course that the church today does not adhere literally to these criteria for males in church leadership. Again, this exercise of selective or arbitrary adherence to different requirements or prohibitions in the very same biblical text then alludes more to prevailing sociocultural paradigms and comfort zones, rather than the adherence to what we believe are non-changeable doctrinal truths and principles.

We do not usually debate whether God would make an *exception* to choose as the future king the young boy David, who for all intents and purposes appeared to be considered the least of the children in his father Jesse's eyes. No, we see this as a concrete example and understanding of how God would choose anyone, including someone who at that young age is not outwardly recognised yet as a great leader and warrior. And yet we seemingly have endless debates and discussions about Deborah's leadership story, or Priscilla's act of teaching a male, as an *exception* to the rule, rather than a further confirmation of God's modus operandi – that God chooses whom he wills, even those considered to be the least or last for the task, and that a person's background, social status or gender are not pre-eminent discriminatory criteria that inform God's choices and decisions. The story of the Samaritan woman who evangelised much of her community, males and females alike, is also testament to this.

The hitherto resistance to the acceptance of these stories and actions of women just as we read them in the bible is telling, because it reveals the already biased lens through which these debates are conducted, skewing the debate about women's calling right from the start. The starting point should not be how the stories of women fit or make sense in relation to the familiar paradigm of thought and belief we routinely employ (even subconsciously), but rather how all such biblical examples of men and women inform and develop our understanding of God's agenda, his kingdom and his will.

Relevance of restrictions across biblical scriptures

If we are to take Paul's words in the books of 1 Timothy 2: 11-12 literally and apply that as a universal prohibition for women, then we'd be obliged to place women-specific caveats across the entire scriptures in the Bible – in scriptures that instruct believers on running their race, working out their calling, loving and serving God with their whole being, and in scriptures on the responsibilities, authority and requirements of discipleship in the Great Commission. For example, Paul instructs believers:

> '*Therefore, since we are surrounded by such a great cloud of witnesses, let us throw off everything that hinders and the sin that so easily entangles. And let us run with perseverance the race marked out for us, fixing our eyes on Jesus, the pioneer and perfecter of faith*'. [19]

So in applying such women-specific caveats for women, we should then say that men are to run their race with determination and perseverance aiming to win, serving God and all God's people with all of their soul, heart and might. The race is apparently only marked out fully for men. Women however should apply a caveat to this instruction and should run their race only in certain lanes in limited activities, roles and positions that are non-leading or influential - they should remain in secondary, support roles and activities largely aimed at just half of God's people. That's not running the race as a disciple with your whole being, with all that you are and have in you. Neither is it full devotion and complete submission in worship to God. And this is certainly not understood to be indicated in Paul's instruction here.

So what does Paul mean to convey?

The 1st century church grappled with many challenges related to traditions and religious laws as they navigated the new way of the ecclesia for 1st century converts, such as the issue of circumcision[20] for followers who now came from both Jewish and Gentile backgrounds. In this case Paul took an adaptive approach[21] so as to not hinder the evangelisation of unbelievers and to avoid misunderstanding among the diverse new believers. Even though Paul was circumcised and instructed Timothy to be circumcised, he nevertheless taught that neither circumcision nor uncircumcision affects a believer's relationship with the Lord, and that outwardly obedience in keeping to the law has no merit in itself. This is because the converted believer is received by God because of his faith in Christ's ultimate atonement, rather than because of good works. Paul extols the believers struggling with this issue to keep running their race as follows:

> '*For in Christ Jesus neither circumcision nor uncircumcision has any value. The only thing that counts is faith expressing itself through love.*
>
> *You were running a good race. Who cut in on you to keep you from obeying the truth? That kind of persuasion does not come from the one who calls you.*'[22]

The evidence throughout scriptures that women did indeed serve as leaders and teach men within the body of believers, and received not only the praise of fellow believers, including Paul, but also enjoyed God's blessing, thus stands in direct contrast to a perceived blanket prohibition of this taken from a few select biblical passages. Then what are we to deduce when Paul states in the letters to the believers in Ephesus and Corinth that women should be silent and not teach[23]?

Just as Paul takes a particular approach with regards to circumcision, could it be plausible to deduce that the seemingly contrasting instructions are given within the unique context of particular challenges related to conduct and behavior faced in those Ephesian and Corinthian churches at that time?

Rather than it being a universal doctrine or principle for all churches, could Paul's approach here too relate to the protection of the gospel - to avoid misunderstanding and negative spiritual impact on new believers which could hinder the sharing of the gospel in those particular churches?

The mission of the contemporary church

Since this is indeed a spiritual cause we are all engaged in, what therefore is left for us to understand as the spiritual imperative to continue to arbitrarily advocate that the most senior or most visible roles in God's kingdom advancement are for the preferential access and privilege of one half of the created image bearers of God?

The church today is in fact largely female - 65% of UK and 61% of US (estimated 66% worldwide) regular church attendees are women[24]. Data shows that 87%-90% of senior leadership positions in the contemporary church are appointed from the minority pool of males[25] who make up 34% of church attendees, with reports of increasing burnout and attrition among church leaders.

This is an ecclesia shackled and restrained, hobbling towards what it believes is its dominion mandate end goal. Not an ecclesia running the race of kingdom advancement at full pace, in unity and solidarity, face set like flint, in the full power of its entire body.

All of this often leaves Christian women who are left standing on the side lines confused, wondering, '***Whose race are we running anyway?***'[26]

CHAPTER 13

The Time is Now

Jesus ushered in a new covenant that empowered women, in contrast to the human cultural understanding of the time. This new covenant is still a work in progress even today and has as yet not reached its full realization. Under the old covenant Jewish priests ministered on behalf of the people of God, who themselves had no direct access to God. Jesus ended this need for the old covenant priesthood, when he sacrificed himself once for all men and women, reconciling us to God, so that we now all have access rights to God. Jesus became our High Priest and we his people, men and women, became a holy priesthood[1].

Therefore, the new covenant expression of old covenant priesthood is now not to be found in positional roles in the temple, but rather it is to be found in the ecclesia as a whole. Called out and set apart Christian men and women occupying the marketplaces and societies across the globe are all now included in the priesthood of believers.

Whose race are we running?

Jesus recruited the leaders for his ecclesia from the marketplace, not the temples or religious institutions of the day. The 120 disciples that prayed together and received the Holy Spirit on Pentecost were largely a group of women and men from the marketplace.

And today we ask ourselves, what and where is the ecclesia? Where are we salt and light? Where and with whom do we share the gospel truths? And how does our narrow paradigm of spiritual authority, hierarchy and designated role exclusivity fit into the command for us to go out in this world and influence it, minister wherever and in whichever context we may find ourselves, and make disciples of all men and women, bringing them to salvation? How does it fit with Jesus' command for us to love God and serve him wholeheartedly with all that we are and have – our whole heart, soul, mind and strength?[2]

The 1st century church faced this challenge from the religious leaders who occupied the ordained offices within the Jewish religious structures of the day. In Acts 4: 1-20 we read that Peter and John were courageously preaching and teaching in the marketplace[3]. When the priests and Sadducees saw these '*unschooled, ordinary men*'[4] they tried to silence them publicly by challenging them regarding whose authority they were teaching under, since they were not teaching and discipling others inside the temples or synagogues under the authority of the religious leaders of the day. Perhaps the institutionalized paradigms of understanding, tradition, culture and power dynamics within the temple and synagogue walls limited the ability or willing of those serving within them to engage in a way that brought them new understanding and revelation, a renewing of the mind[5].

In explaining their great commission to go out into all the world, the disciples in response chose to highlight the superior authority of Jesus under whose name they were preaching[6],

> '*Which is right in God's eyes: to listen to you, or to God? You be the judges! As for us,* ***we cannot help speaking about what we have seen and heard.***'

Due to the transformative shift and new life that Jesus ushered in through his sacrifice for us all on the cross and the inclusion of *every* believer into the priesthood, this too should be the approach and understanding among all believers today, male and female.

> ***We cannot be silent, for we cannot help speaking about what we have seen, heard and now know.***

Hidden in plain sight

Jesus intended the ecclesia to be like salt and light[7] – something that permeates, influences, modifies and transforms for the better, ushering in a righteous state of being. And that is our role in the outworking of our calling in the marketplace ministry of God.

In contrast, a highly contained and controlled institutionalized church is often at risk of being inert and thus less effective or impactful. It is in the phase of commissioning within its organisational structure that the church has taken on the role of gatekeeper for God's outworking of the Great Commission, by restricting the areas into which women may be commissioned. A church that acts as gatekeeper to the full expression of the Holy Spirit power within the majority (66%) of its global community of believers, profoundly limits its transformative power in the world.

Such gatekeeping behaviour keeps women contained in stereotypes and models of identity that were never God's intention, and that do not fit women as they truly and fully are. Neither does it fit a world in which women are present everywhere within the marketplace, making valuable contributions and meeting the needs of their children and society as a whole.

> ***God's power embodied in the female image bearers within the Body of Christ has been hidden in plain sight for generations.***

For centuries women and girls have lived with the awareness of the potential they know is inside of them, irrespective of the cultural paradigms that have dictated what women may or may not do or accomplish. How much longer does the church wish to act as gatekeeper to the release of the power, gifting and anointing of God which He has placed within the women in the church?

We are commanded to run the race fully, not half-heartedly, or partially, or even overly cautiously because we are fearful – the parable of the buried talent would attest to that[8]. We are commanded to be fruitful and multiply, not only in the physical sense, but also in the spiritual sense. Women should have equitable opportunity and access to pursue their calling and exercise their gifting as fully and powerfully as they can through and with God. Can we truly answer with conviction that we know the mind and intention of Christ if we continue to argue for an approach that suppresses the work of the Holy Spirit in the lives of those God has called, and restricts the opportunity for all believers, male and female alike, to run their race fully for the advancement of God's kingdom?

We should not misunderstand what we, the ecclesia, are here for. It is out of the outpouring of the Spirit in and through the Body of Christ that the world is transformed in whichever spheres of influence Christian believers find themselves.

Righteous spiritual and social transformation can become a reality when each of us come to terms with how we uphold practices and beliefs that are limiting, damaging and unjust, and which hold back the full manifestation and impact of the Holy Spirit through all believers in the ecclesia.

Holding any part of our human and spiritual potential back, limits what's possible with God. Imagine what the ecclesia could have accomplished in generations past and can accomplish still in this increasingly secular generation and beyond when God is left to do what only he can and wants to do in all of us[9], for the outpouring of his full glory on earth. Imagine what life would look like if we stripped everything away, and fully submitted to a holy Messiah - where we are all running our race full out together, going as far as we can with God, as far as he will take us, in whichever sphere of influence we find ourselves. Imagine what a powerful impact that would have on the earth! A new wine poured into a new wineskin[10].

> ***For out of the home flows the ramifications for our society and our future.***
>
> ***And out of the church culture, will and belief systems flows the righteous impact on the society and the world.***

God is calling his ecclesia, the body of believers, into the marketplaces and societies across the globe. God continues to use men and women who are willing to trust God and obey[11], and whose eyes are fixed resolutely on him who is the ultimate and only finisher and perfecter of our faith. Men and women who are not conformed to this world and its understanding, but who are all willing to go wherever, and into whichever spheres of life and society God calls them to. Men and women who understand that this is first and foremost a spiritual battle, not a battle based on human understanding, natural ability or cultural comfort zones.

For such a time as this

An ecclesia that is largely female is already out there in the marketplaces, on the streets, in the workplaces, in homes across the cities and nations, on public platforms and in positions of authority in secular society. Workers in the harvest field. Being salt and light wherever they find themselves. Just as Esther, Deborah, Miriam and Mary recognised the role they could and should play in their generation, so too women today have been predestined by God to be born into this generation, because they too are positioned by him to be the righteous solution for the challenges this generation faces.

Since the Fall the sons and daughters of God have been on a slow journey in their evolution of understanding of what God's divine design and mandate for us is, and how God wants us to walk out our calling in a fallen and broken world. An exercise in bravely and boldly *unlearning and relearning.* A challenging process the 12 disciples and then the 1st century church had to go through in order to come to a new and fresh understanding of God's love and Jesus' mission on earth - to make God the Father, his character and his will known, and to redeem us all from our sins. An unlearning and relearning which the Pharisees, the religious leaders of the day, struggled to comprehend or do.

Since the Day of Pentecost the church itself has wrestled and continues to wrestle with the practical outworking of this new understanding of the ecclesia's mandate within this level playing field - where God's Spirit is poured out and works powerfully for the fulfilment of the Great Commission through *all* who accept the salvation of Jesus Christ[12]. And what it means to be justified by faith, and to fully walk in freedom under the grace of God as sons and daughters of Abraham and co-heirs of the promise.

At the time of the 1st century church the culture was patriarchal, women did not have the religious, social and other educational advantage that men had enjoyed for generations, slavery was accepted as part of the lives of those in the church community, and the church's overseers were Jewish and male. The 1st century church faced making sense of what it meant practically where men and women of various ethnic, cultural and prior religious and other backgrounds were now included without discrimination and on equal footing in the body of believers and in God's kingdom mandate. A liberating and unifying salvation mandate of ethnic, social and gender equality in which there is neither[13]

1. Jew nor Gentile
2. Slave nor free
3. Male nor female

Neither Jew nor Gentile

The bible includes stories of non-Jewish people who were conscripted into the plans and purposes of God and assimilated into the Jewish people. Women like the Gentile converts Ruth and Rahab who were included in the genealogy of Jesus. Another example is that of the Samaritan woman at the well, who evangelised most of her fellow Samaritans in her village - both females and uncircumcised males were accepted by Jesus as believers under Christ's salvation.

The 1st century church leaders nevertheless wrestled with how they were to understand the outworking of their faith and the previously applied Jewish religious laws, now that non-Jews who did not come from the same traditions, were included in the Body of Christ.

One example was the issue of circumcision[14], as we've discussed before. Another example in Acts 10: 1-48 was Peter's dilemma regarding entering the home of a Gentile and eating with them[15], an act that would have been seen as unclean in the Jewish culture and religious law. God challenged Peter's understanding of what is appropriate and acceptable before God, with Peter ultimately declaring that '*God does not show favoritism but accepts from every nation the one who fears him and does what is right.*'

The 1st century disciples paid with their lives in pursuit of this, bringing the gospel to people of all races, ethnicities and religious heritages, Jews and Gentiles alike, '*in Jerusalem and in all Judea and Samaria, and to the ends of the earth*'. And as believers today we are all beneficiaries of this egalitarian conviction.

Neither slave nor free

The Christian church addressed and abolished discrimination against non-Jews right from the start at the birth of the 1st century church, but it took another 1000+ years from the Day of Pentecost before the global church fully acknowledged and decisively addressed the discriminatory injustice of slavery within society and within its own body.

History has shown the church's complicity and its material gain from the slave trade. Christianisation of slaves was often employed to achieve their compliance[16]. Even though slavery was commonly accepted in the 1st century, and it indeed still exists today, nobody in the contemporary Christian church would consider it biblically sound to advocate for the continued subjugation of other human beings in this way, or to consider it a prescriptive principle on which to build and lead the contemporary church.

At the 2006 debate of the General Synod of the Church of England the then Archbishop of Canterbury, Rowan Williams, acknowledged the Church's corporate and ancestral guilt in regards to slavery as follows[17]:

> "*The Body of Christ is not just a body that exists at any one time; it exists across history and we therefore share the shame and the sinfulness of our predecessors, and part of what we can do, with them and for them in the Body of Christ, is prayerful acknowledgment of the failure that is part of us, not just of some distant 'them*'".

> "*To speak here of repentance and apology is not words alone; it is part of our witness to the Gospel, to a world that needs to hear that the past must be faced and healed and cannot be ignored ... by doing so we are actually discharging our responsibility to preach good news, not simply to look backwards in awkwardness and embarrassment, but to speak of the freedom we are given to face ourselves, including the unacceptable regions of... our history.*"

Neither male nor female

Today we continue on this dynamic journey in the evolution of our understanding, this journey of wrestling, of unlearning and relearning what it means for all God's children to be unequivocally under the covenant and promise of God.

And so today, over 2000 years since the liberating act of Jesus' birth, death and resurrection that has included us all in the promises of God as co-heirs with Christ, we wrestle still with the last section of Paul's profound statement, '*neither male nor female*'.

None of our position, inheritance, responsibility or authority as believers in Christ is declared in the Bible as a gender-based privilege. God's desire is for men and women to stand in dignity alongside each other before him, in mutuality and equitable partnership, and as co-heirs seated with Christ to bring forth God's kingdom and reign with him in eternity[18].

We've come a long way since the lowly socio-cultural status, role and standing of women that was prevalent at the time of the 1st century church, or the beliefs about the inferiority of women to be educated at all that were prevalent during the Renaissance[19] (based then on the interpretations of 1 Timothy 2: 11-12). We see increasing examples today of gifted and anointed female Christian teachers and leaders, no longer invisible in the annals of history, but running the race that God has set before them, fulfilling the prophetic utterance of Psalm 68:11:

> '*The Lord announces the word, and the women who **proclaim** it are a mighty throng (army).*'

Before one may be tempted to diminish the significance of this act of proclamation by this mighty throng of women, it should be noted that the Hebrew word for '*proclaim*' used here in Psalm 68:11 is *basar* (בָּשַׂר)[20]. This same word, *basar*, is also used when talking about Jesus' actions in Isaiah 61:1 which Jesus himself confirmed when he read this scripture in the temple at age twelve:

> '*The Spirit of the Sovereign LORD is on me, because the Lord has anointed me to proclaim (basar) good news to the poor.*'

King David's incredible prophetic Old Testament utterance in Psalm 68 pointed to Jesus' restorative mission and God's divine purpose for women in the latter days. The same proclamation of good news that Jesus does, women are prophetically called to do also!

Could it be that for such a time as this in these latter days, more than 2000 years after Paul uttered the words 'neither male nor female' at the Day of Pentecost, that God is challenging the ecclesia to take up its mandate fully, and to throw off the shackles that hinder the full outpouring of his power and glory? This is the consideration we are left with today.

CHAPTER 14

The Final Battle

Rise Up

Rise up Woman of God
You've been on your knees long enough
Rise up Woman of God
You Holy Priesthood
You Saints of God
Rise up Woman of God

Woman of God, God knows you and calls you by name. Long before you were formed in your mother's womb, long before the world told you who you are, God knew you and he called you to his purposes[1]. Women played prominent and significant roles in God's redemptive plan throughout the Bible. We have explored the stories of countless women in the scriptures, named and unnamed, who have demonstrated and showcased how God has and continues to use, elevate and empower women for his calling and his purposes. Ordinary women just like you and I who left their mark in the annals of history because of what an extraordinary God did through them. And it is the same today. There is a place in God's mandate for you. He has a calling for you.

The devil also knows who you are, *in part*. Woman of God, you are in a spiritual battle of the ages, a longstanding enmity between you and the ruler of this world. Your enemy Satan roams about like a roaring lion, looking for whom he may devour. Throughout human history Satan has worked hard to diminish the identity, role and legitimacy of women both spiritually and societally. What

Satan fears is men and women working in full partnership, in the full power of the Holy Spirit. Because when this happens, and women operate in the full power God intended for them, what they would birth together would result in Satan's crushing.

Unless you know and stand firm in your God-ordained identity and calling, and your authority in Christ, you are weakened on the battlefield.

> ***But when a woman remembers who she is, the battle changes.***
>
> ***It wholly, completely and utterly changes.***

Because when women remember whose they are, who they are made to be and what they are made for, the game changes[2]. You are not an orphan walking through a meaningless desert with no one knowing exactly who you are or the authority you hold in this earthly life. No ma'am! You are the daughter of the King. You have heaven's authority as an adopted child[3], as co-heir with Christ[4], as a royal priesthood[5], and as God's ecclesia, his righteous governance here on earth. The creator in whose image you are created has loved you with an everlasting love since the creation of earth and he calls you his own. When we understand our decisive calling in and unto God, everything we believe, say, do and have is invested with compelling devotion, passion and purpose. We need to own and walk in this truth.

Let us allow God to use what he has already entrusted to us and placed in us as women. God is doing a new thing[6] all around us and we better perceive it. He is breaking down strongholds and yolks of bondage. Whatever enmity the devil has meant for evil, God uses for his good[7]. God has placed women on the frontlines of the spiritual battle, as protagonists in his redemption story. Women are prophetically called and commissioned to proclaim the gospel to all and display his glory to the ends of the earth. And the bible tells us that the women who walk in this calling, are a mighty throng, a mighty army.

> '*The Lord announces the word, and the women who proclaim it are a* ***mighty throng***'[8]

Woman, you are a warrior in the army of God! You come from a long line of warriors in the bible. The devil is a defeated foe. God has already won the victory! The first defeat of Satan came when Jesus defeated death on the cross and paid the price for all sin. The final defeat will come in the last days, when the army of God on earth will march forward in victory and the final return of Christ will take place. That knowledge is power.

We need to regain the same sense of urgency of the 1st century church where all Spirit-filled, gifted and willing disciples of Christ are liberated, equipped and sent out as a mighty army. There's too much at stake. The battle is real.

So take up your sword woman of God. Put on the armour of God[9] and fight the good fight[10]. Walk forward, in strength and in your rightful identity. God is raising up his army in these latter days and he wants you to be part of the battle. He's calling you to the frontline.

Woman take up your mantle and go forth confidently wherever and however God chooses, unlimited and not influenced by a worldly understanding. Trust in God's understanding and his ways. Commit your plans and actions to God[11]. Dare to audaciously believe and hope in a God to whom the earth and all its laws are subject. God has equipped you and continues to equip and empower you, just like the women in the bible.

God never gives us an assignment he knows is not meant for us or that is not possible to accomplish with him. At the Fall when God placed us in direct battle with the devil, he knew exactly who we were. He knew exactly what we as women can and will accomplish with him.

So take up your sword woman! Stand upright and claim your place. Stop occupying a place of unknown or mistaken identity, an identity that was never ascribed to you by God. Woman, you were created a vital, powerful part of the mandate given by God – an *ezer* of strength and competence. Fearfully and wonderfully made. You have been called by name by the One who sees things that aren't and says they are. Don't live a lesser version of yourself, of what God has created you to be. You are more than a mother or wife. There is more in you and for you than just secondary service on the sidelines, in the background, as a supportive backup. Woman rise up and take your rightful place.

A Woman's Place

Woman, know your place!
The place of a woman is everywhere
In the fulfilment of the dominion mandate
In the birthing of the Messiah
In the great commission of the Christian church
In the advancement of the kingdom of God on earth
In the final battle to overcome Satan

So take up your baton, your mantle, and run woman!
Run as far and hard as you can, run like there's no tomorrow
Run your God-given race unfettered, unlimited, purposed
Run like the world depended on it
Run like you don't depend on the world and its opinion
Put your face like flint, straining towards the goal
Woman, know your place, run your race!

Woman, know your place! Your place is everywhere. In the home, in the church of God, in society, in the marketplace, on the frontlines and in the advancement of God's kingdom. Your mission field is where you live, study, work, play and worship. Everywhere.

It's time to see yourself the way God does. Fix your eyes solidly on Jesus, the author and perfecter of your faith[12]. You were born for this. Be bold. Be determined. Persevere. Run your race full out and live a life worthy of the calling you have received[13].

There is too much at stake. The souls of many are at stake. The impact of the church as difference makers is at stake. The righteous transformation of our societies is at stake.

There is too much at stake for us to squander away precious time, resources, dreams, desires, gifts and energy on trying to maintain and uphold a status quo that has no basis in the example and teachings of Jesus and the scriptures about our shared identity, calling, inheritance and authority.

Imagine a world where ....communities thrive because every member of that community is equally valued. Where women are not a problem, but are championed as a powerful solution. Where every girl and boy deserves the opportunity to develop the potential that is inside of them. Where girls and boys believe they can live a life of significance. Where marriage partnership in the home is commonly understood to be one of mutual submission, honor, love, respect and other-centredness.

Imagine an ecclesia where ...... our children learn that in God's providence heroes of the faith are not largely male by default. Where no one hears a message that they should restrict the full exercise of their spiritual gifts. Where no one hears the message that that they should limit where and how far they pursue their calling in the advancement of the kingdom. Where women's voices are valued the way God values women's voices. Where no believer is silent, but they are compelled to speak because of what they've seen, heard and know of God and his goodness[14]. Where for the joy set before them, men and women are running the race together, in unity and solidarity, full out and with no limits.

It's time for each believer, including each and every woman, to actively and intentionally pursue their personal calling for the sake of the kingdom and out of obedience to our Creator and Redeemer.

Jesus (the master) rebukes the servant who hides his talent and gives the most praise to the servant who has been the most fruitful with the talents given[15]. So too, settling for a lesser life than that to which we are called as women is not what God is satisfied with.

It's no accident that you find yourself where you are. God has placed you there, whether for a season or a lifetime. For such a time as this. For his highest purpose. For his glory.

It's time that women courageously step up and step in to the calling and power of God in them. It's time that men and women alike acknowledge that '*it is not good for man to be alone*'[16].

It's time for the members of God's global ecclesia[17] to serve the body of Christ according to the grace of their salvation and their gifting, calling and anointing, rather than on any other selection criteria or association. When the called and anointed believers, irrespective of gender, are appropriately commissioned, the impact of God's power is manifest.

God calls us not to love our life, the status quo, our allegiances or our comfort zones so much that we are not willing to die[18] to that, in order to take hold of the promise that God has for us. We should not be intimidated by the lies of the devil. Because what God has for us is so much more.

The full release of both men and women into their calling and Holy Spirit power is the story of restoration in God's kingdom[19].

Righteous spiritual and social transformation can become a reality when each of us come to terms with how we uphold practices and beliefs that are limiting, damaging and unjust, and which hold back the full manifestation and impact of the Holy Spirit through all believers in the ecclesia. Silence and inaction is collusion.

Let us stand up and be counted in our generation, adding our voice, time and resources to activities and initiatives that promote the potential and whole identity of girls and women. Let the leadership teams of church organisations intentionally cultivate a culture of active nurturing, equipping, encouragement and empowerment of the men and women in their congregations alike. Let us champion a positive approach to how all, male and female, can collaboratively grow, work together and live out their full potential and calling.

We cannot do this life, and run our race, without God and without each other[20]. God wants to partner with us, working with and co-creating with us to establish his kingdom on earth. With the great crowd of witnesses that have gone before, let us put aside every encumbrance and together let us run the race that God has set before us[21]. Greater is he and his purposes in us than anyone or anything that is in the world[22]. All of creation is waiting with eager expectation for the children of God to be revealed[23].

For those women who have drunk from the cup of disappointment and crushed hope, be encouraged today. You can make a new start from the rubble[24]. Beauty can come from ashes. Dry bones can come to life. You can gain a new perspective amidst uncertainty. Chains can be broken. Familial patterns can be shattered. Oppression and injustice can be removed.

Arise and shine woman of God, for your light has come[25]. Let go of the past[26]. Step out of the narrative that has held you back. Stretch your tent pegs wide[27]. Whether you are young, old, single, married, a stay-at-home mother or wife, or a mother or wife that also has a formal occupation outside the home - you are never too *whatever* to be used by God. God has and will continue to elevate and commission women from every background in extraordinary ways for his glory. Stand firm in your faith and the faith of your biblical ancestors, confident in the things you hope for and the things not yet seen[28]. Woman of God persist, push through and run your race, not as one who suffers or tolerates, but as a warrior!

The life that Jesus offers us as co-heirs and as his royal priesthood is so much more than we can imagine[29]. Celebrate all that you bring to God's table – your femininity, compassion, love, nurturing, intellect, intuition, skill, emotions, spiritual gifts, fortitude, steadfastness, strength and wisdom – all of it! Bring it and celebrate it. Do not let the cultural norms of the day allow you to settle for less than that which God has prepared for you long ago. Life is more than just going through life following a routine or meeting societal expectations. Blessed rather are those who hear God and obey.

God designed each one of us for a life of purpose and significance. You were born with God's unique imprint on you, an original. Do not live and die a copy of someone else's idea of who you are. The world cannot afford it. The harvest is ripe. The final battle, the battle of the ages, is at hand. The restoration of God's kingdom is at hand. Take the next small step in your calling with boldness and confidence in the God you serve. Step into the new story you are willing to co-create with God[30].

Woman of God, rise up. For such a time as this and for this generation, God has called YOU.

THE CALL OF A WOMAN

The Call of A Woman is Strong
The Call of A Woman is Vital
The Call of A Women is Powerful
The Call of A Woman is God-Ordained

The Call of A Woman is a Song from Days of Old
The Call of a Woman is a Battle Cry
The Call of A Woman is a Roar and a Shout
The Call of A Woman is a Voice Across the Ages

The Call of a Woman is Essential in Battle
The Call of a Woman is on the Frontlines
The Call of a Woman is a Call to Action
The Call of a Woman is of a Mighty Warrior

The Call of a Woman is one of Mutual Partnership
The Call of a Woman is a Needed Part of Christ's Body
The Call of a Woman is Everywhere, in Every Place
The Call of a Woman is Irrevocable

Notes

Part 1: Women's God-Given Identity and Calling

Introduction – The Race and Calling

1. Heb 12: 1-2; Acts 20:24; Ps 119: 32; 2 Tim 4:7; 1 Cor 9: 24; Prov 4:25; Phil 3:14
2. Gal 5: 7-8
3. https://www.merriam-webster.com/dictionary/calling
4. John 3: 16-17; Ps 111:9; Is 44: 21-23; Lam 3:58
5. Eph 1: 3–14; 2 Tim 1:9; 1 Thess 4:7; 1 Peter 2:9; 1 John 4:19; Jer 31:3; Eph 1: 4-5; John 15:16
6. Deut 6:4–5; Matt 22:36–37; Mark 12:30
7. Matt 22: 39; Matt 28:19-20
8. Matt 16: 16-19; Luke 4: 16-18; https://biblehub.com/greek/1577.htm
9. https://biblehub.com/greek/1577.htm
10. https://ekklesiaeverywhere.com/about/whatisekklesia/ https://www.bibletools.org/index.cfm/fuseaction/Topical.show/RTD/cgg/ID/2415/Ekklesia.htm
11. Eph 2:10; Eph 2:19; 1 John 3:1; Zeph 3:17; 2 Cor 5:17; 2 Cor 5:21; 1 Peter 2:9
12. Matt 18:20
13. Eccl 3:1-8
14. Ps 139: 13; 1 Thess 2:12; Is 43:1-4
15. Eph 1: 3–14; Jer 1: 5
16. Num 23:19; 2 Cor 1:20

Chapter 1: In the Beginning

1. Genesis 5:2; Gen 1: 27
2. Gen 1: 26-30
3. Gen 2:8; Gen 2:15
4. Gen 2: 16-17
5. Gen 2: 18
6. Gen 2: 19
7. Gen 2: 20
8. Gen 2: 23; Gen 5:2
9. Gen 1:31
10. Gen 1: 28-30
11. https://biblehub.com/hebrew/5828.htm
    https://hebrewwordlessons.com/2018/05/13/helper-defining-the-ezer-woman/
    https://www.ancient-hebrew.org/studies-interpretation/what-is-a-help-meet.htm
12. Gen 2: 18, Gen 2: 20
13. Is 30:5; Ez 12:14; Dan 11:34
14. Ex 18:4; Deut 33:7; Deut 33:26; Deut 33:29; Ps 20:2; Ps 33:20; ; Ps 70:5; Ps 89:19; Ps 115:9; Ps 115:10; Ps 115:11; Ps 121:1; Ps 121:2; Ps 124:8; Ps 146:5; Hos 13:9
15. Gen 1: 28
16. 1 Cor 11:11-12
17. Gen 3:20

Chapter 2: The Fall

1. Gen 3: 1
2. Gen 3:6
3. Gen 3: 16
4. Gen 3: 16-19; Gen 3: 23
5. Silvoso, Ed (2010) Women: God's secret weapon – God's inspiring message to women of power, purpose and destiny. Chosen Books.

Chapter 3: A World out of Balance

1. https://www.droit-humain.org/womens-education-rights-history/#from%2020th%20Century%20Till%20Today
2. https://en.wikipedia.org/wiki/1_Timothy_2:12
3. https://www.insider.com/when-women-around-the-world-got-the-right-to-vote-2019-2
4. https://en.wikipedia.org/wiki/Women%27s_property_rights
   https://historyswomen.com/miscellaneous-articles/property-rights-of-women/
   https://www.theguardian.com/money/us-money-blog/2014/aug/11/women-rights-money-timeline-history
5. https://www.land-links.org/issue-brief/fact-sheet-land-tenure-womens-empowerment/
6. https://www.nationalgeographic.com/culture/article/partner-content-empowering-female-farmers
7. https://www.fao.org/3/i2050e/i2050e02.pdf
8. https://www.fao.org/3/i2050e/i2050e02.pdf
9. Kristoff, N D and WuDunn, S (2008) Half the Sky: Turning Oppression into Opportunity for Women Worldwide. Published by Knopf.
10. United Nations Office on Drugs and Crime (2018) Global Study on Homicide: Gender related killing of women and girls. https://www.unodc.org/documents/data-and-analysis/GSH2018/GSH18_Gender-related_killing_of_women_and_girls.pdf
11. Honour Based Violence Awareness Network, International Resource Centre, Honour Based Violence Statistics. http://hbv-awareness.com/statistics-data/
12. https://www.who.int/en/news-room/fact-sheets/detail/violence-against-women
13. http://documents.worldbank.org/curated/en/489381468740165817/pdf/multi0page.pdf
14. https://www.nytimes.com/2013/11/07/us/reports-of-military-sexual-assault-rise-sharply.html
15. https://www.who.int/en/news-room/fact-sheets/detail/female-genital-mutilation

16. https://documents1.worldbank.org/curated/en/926401524803880673/pdf/125804-PUB-REPLACEMENT-PUBLIC.pdf
17. https://www.unwomen.org/sites/default/files/Headquarters/Attachments/Sections/Library/Publications/2018/SDG-report-Fact-sheet-Global-en.pdf
http://www3.weforum.org/docs/GGGR16/WEF_Global_Gender_Gap_Report_2016.pdf
18. https://www.unwomen.org/sites/default/files/Headquarters/Attachments/Sections/Library/Publications/2018/SDG-report-Fact-sheet-Global-en.pdf
19. http://www.independent.co.uk/life-style/husbands-create-extra-seven-hours-of-housework-a-week-a6885951.html
https://theconversation.com/census-2016-women-are-still-disadvantaged-by-the-amount-of-unpaid-housework-they-do-76008
20. https://www.ilo.org/wcmsp5/groups/public/---dgreports/---inst/documents/publication/wcms_557077.pdf
https://www.bls.gov/opub/ted/2015/time-spent-in-leisure-activities-in-2014-by-gender-age-and-educational-attainment.htm
21. https://fortune.com/2023/01/12/fortune-500-companies-ceos-women-10-percent/
22. https://www.unwomen.org/en/digital-library/publications/2021/03/women-in-politics-map-2021
23. Perez, Caroline Criado (2020). Invisible Women. Random House.
24. https://www.thebalancemoney.com/do-companies-with-female-executives-perform-better-4586443#citation-1
25. https://www.catalyst.org/wp-content/uploads/2019/01/The_Bottom_Line_Connecting_Corporate_Performance_and_Gender_Diversity.pdf
26. John 16:33

Part 2: Women's Calling Throughout the Scriptures

Chapter 4: The Role of Women in the Old Testament

1. Deut 29: 9-12
2. Josh 8:34-35
3. Deut. 31:12
4. 1 Sam 1:12
5. Ps 68: 24-25
6. Ex 35: 25; Ruth 2:7; 1Sam 8: 13
7. Prov 31
8. Gen 29
9. Gen 35:19; Gen 23:19; Gen 35:8; Gen 49: 31
10. Ex 15:1-21; Micah 6: 4; 1 Chron 6:3
11. Gen 11:29-31; Gen 12:5-17; Gen 16:1-8; Gen 17:15-21; Gen 18; Gen 20:2-18; Gen 21:1-12; Gen 23:1-19; Gen 24:36, Gen 37; Gen 25:10-12; Gen 49:31; Heb 11:11
12. Gen 16
13. Judges 4-5
14. Judges 4: 17-23
15. 2 Kings 22:14-20; 2 Chron 34:22-28
16. Is 8:3; https://claudemariottini.com/2013/08/23/isaiahs-wife/
17. Book of Esther
18. 2 Kings 11; 2 Chron 22: 10-12
19. 1 Sam 1:2–2:21
20. 1 Sam 25:14-45; 1 Chron 3
21. 2 Sam 20:14-22
22. Numb 27: 1-11; Numb 36; Josh 17:3
23. Numb 36:2-8
24. Job 42: 15
25. Numb 26: 33
26. Matt 1:1-17
27. Gen 38; Ruth 4:11-12
28. Josh 2: 1-3, Josh 6: 17-25; Heb 11:31
29. Ruth 4:9-17

30. 2 Sam 11:1-3; 2 Sam 12:24; 1 Kings 1:11-16, 1 Kings 1: 28-31; 1 Kings 2:13-19; 1 Chron 3:5; Ps 51:1
31. Isa 7:14; Micah 5:2-3; Matt 1:23; Gal. 4:4; Luke 1: 46-55
32. Job 42: 1-2
33. Numb 23:19; Heb 13: 8

Chapter 5: Jesus and the Calling of Women

1. https://jewsforjesus.org/publications/newsletter/newsletter-jun-1988/jesus-and-the-role-of-women/
2. Luke 11: 27-28
3. John 8
4. Luke 13:10-17
5. Gal 3:27-29
6. Mark 5:24-34; Luke 8:43-48; Matt 9:20-22
7. Levi 15:25-27
8. Luke 7: 36-50
9. Luke 10:38-42; John 12:1-8
10. John 4: 7-42
11. Matt 1: 1-17
12. Luke 1: 26-45
13. Luke 2:36-38
14. John 2: 1-11
15. John 4: 1-42
16. Mark 7: 24-30
17. John 4: 10; John 4: 25-26
18. John 11:21-27
19. Luke 24:1-8; Matt 28: 1-6
20. Matt 28: 9-10; John 20:14-18
21. Luke 24:9; Matt 28: 9-10; John 20:14-18; Mark 16: 1-10
22. Luke 2:1-20; John 19: 25-27; Acts 1: 12-14
23. Matt 12: 46-50; Matt 27:55; Mark 15:40-41; Luke 8:19-21
24. Luke 10: 38-42
25. Mark 15: 41
26. Matt 26: 6-13; Mark 14: 3-9; John 12: 1-3

27. Luke 8:1-3
28. Luke 8:2; Luke 24:10; John 19:25; John 20: 1-2; John 20:11; John 20: 18; Mark 15:40; Mark 15:47; Mark 16:1; Mark 16:9; Matt 27:56; Matt 27:61; Matt 28:1
29. Luke 15:8-10
30. Matt 13:33; Luke 13:21
31. Luke 18:1-8
32. Matt 25:1-13
33. Luke 23:28-31
34. Matt 27:55-56; Mark 15:39-41; Luke 23: 49; John 19: 25-27

Chapter 6: The Role of Women in the 1st Century Church

1. Acts 1:12-14
2. Acts 2: 17-18; Joel 2: 28-32
3. Acts 2: 38-39
4. Gal 3: 26-29
5. Rom 11: 29
6. Phil 4:3
7. Acts 1:12-14
8. Acts 2: 1-4
9. Rom 16:1; Rom 16:7; Phil 4: 2-3; Acts 18: 26; Acts 21: 9; 1 Cor 11: 5
10. Acts 8: 3-4
11. Rom 16
12. Rom 16:1-2
13. Rom 16: 7
14. Rom 16:12
15. 1 Cor 4: 12; 1 Cor 15: 10; Phil 2: 16; Col 1: 29; Gal 4: 11; 1 Tim 4: 10
16. Col 4:15
17. 1 Cor 1: 11
18. Phil 4: 2-3
19. 2 John 1: 1
20. Acts 9:36; Acts 17:34
21. Rom 16:13; Rom 16:15

22. Acts 21:8-9
23. Acts 16:13-15; Acts 16: 40
24. 2 Tim 1:5; 2 Tim 3:15
25. Rom 16: 3-5; Acts 18: 2-3; Acts 18:18-19, Acts 18:24-26; 1 Cor 16: 19; 2 Tim 4:19

Part 3: Case Study - The Calling of Mary

Chapter 7: A Woman Called

1. Gen 3: 15
2. Luke 1: 19
3. Luke 1:11; Luke 1:29; Luke2:10
4. Luke 1: 17
5. Luke 1: 26
6. Luke 2: 8-11
7. Luke 2: 13-14
8. Rev 5:11-12; Rev 7: 11-12; Rev 19:6-7
9. Is 14:12; Ez 28:13-19; Rev 12: 7-8
10. Luke 15:7

Chapter 8: Highly Favored

1. Gen 16:10-11; Gen 17:15-19; Luke 1:11–17; Judges 13:3-21
2. Luke 1: 28-29
3. Luke 1: 11- 22
4. Luke 1:38
5. Gen 3: 15
6. Is 7: 14; Micah 5:2-3; Is 9: 6-7
7. Luke 1: 42-45
8. Matt 2: 1-2; Matt 2: 11
9. Luke 2: 10-12; Luke 2: 16
10. Luke 2: 22-38
11. Luke 2: 19

Chapter 9: A Woman's Mandate

1. Luke 1:11–17
2. Matt 1:16

Chapter 10: Partnership in Marriage

1. Matt 1:19
2. Matt 1: 20
3. Matt 1:25
4. Matt 2:13 – 23
5. Matt 13:55
6. Luke 2: 22-39
7. Luke 2: 4
8. Eph 5: 21; Phil 2:3-8
9. Matt 19: 1-12; Mark 10: 5-9
10. Gen 2: 23-24; Gen 1: 26-27
11. Judges 4-5
12. Gen 21:12
13. 1 Sam 25
14. Acts 18:3; Acts 18:19; Acts 18:26; 1 Cor 16:19; Rom 16:5; 2 Tim 4:19

Chapter 11: A Woman of Substance

1. John 2: 1-12
2. Gen 12: 2-3; Gen 15; Gen 17
3. Is 49:15; Is 66:13
4. Song of Sol 8:2; Eph 6:1-3; 2 Tim 1:5; Prov 1:8-9; Deut 5:16; Ez 16:44; Ex 20:12

Part 4: The Call to Women and the Church today

Chapter 12: Women and their Calling in the Church

1. 1 Cor 12: 8-10; 1 Cor 12: 27-31; 1 Cor 13:1-2; Eph. 4:11-12; Rom 12: 6-8; 1 Pet 4: 9
2. Acts 2: 17-18; Joel 2: 28-32
3. I Cor 12: 11
4. 1 Cor 12: 31; I Cor 14: 1; Rom 12: 6-8
5. 1 Tim 2: 11-15; 1 Tim 3: 2-13; 1 Cor 11: 7-12; 1 Cor 14: 34-35; Eph 5: 21-33
6. https://juniaproject.com/1-timothy-2-does-not-ban-women-teaching-having-authority/ https://www.biblegateway.com/resources/nivac-sample/1Tim.2.11-1Tim.2.12
7. Rom 8: 28
8. Acts 2: 17-18; Joel 2: 28-32
9. 1 Cor 14:1-5; Rom 12:6-8
10. 1 Cor 12: 27-31
11. 1 Cor. 11: 5; 1 Cor 14: 1-18
12. Acts 18:24–28
13. Acts 18: 18; Acts 18: 26; Rom 16: 3; 2 Tim 4: 19; Acts 18: 2-3; 1 Cor 16: 19
14. 2 Tim 4:19
15. 1 Tim 2: 9-15; 1 Cor 11: 5; 1 Cor 14: 34
16. https://www.singlefriendlychurch.com/research/yougov
17. Rom 12: 6-8
18. 1 Cor 12: 1
19. Heb 12: 1-2
20. 1 Cor 7:18-20; Acts 15:1; Acts 16:3; Acts 21:21; Rom 2: 29; Rom 4: 9-11; Coll 3:11; Gal 5: 6; Gal 6:12–16; 1 Cor 9:19–23; Rom 14:1-10; 1 Cor 7:17–24
21. https://bibleask.org/what-did-paul-teach-about-circumcision/
22. Gal 5: 6-8
23. 1 Cor 14: 34-35; 1 Tim 2: 12

24. http://news.bbc.co.uk/1/shared/bsp/hi/pdfs/03_04_07_tearfundchurch.pdf
    https://www.biola.edu/blogs/biola-magazine/2006/the-feminization-of-the-church
    https://churchhealthwiki.wordpress.com/2018/05/04/trends-christian-women-in-the-u-s-are-more-religious-than-their-male-counterparts-pewresearch/
25. https://www.zippia.com/pastor-jobs/demographics/
    https://www.barna.com/research/number-of-female-senior-pastors-in-protestant-churches-doubles-in-past-decade/
26. Gal 1:10

Chapter 13: The Time is Now

1. Heb 2:17; Heb 4:14; Heb 5: 1-8; 1 Peter 2:5
2. Deut 6:4–5; Matt 22:36–37; Mark 12:30
3. Acts 4: 1-20, Acts 5: 12-14
4. Acts 4: 13
5. John 3: 1-11; John 11:45-48
6. Acts 4: 19-20
7. Matt 5:13-16
8. Matt 25:24-30
9. Acts 4: 7-20
10. Matt 9:17; Amos 9:13-14
11. Luke 11:28
12. Acts 2: 17-18, Acts 2: 38-39
13. Gal 3: 26-29
14. 1 Cor 7:18-20; Acts 15:1; Acts 16:3; Acts 21:21; Rom 2:29; Rom 4:3, Rom 4: 10-11
15. Acts 10: 1-48
16. https://www.bbc.co.uk/history/british/abolition/church_and_slavery_article_01.shtml
17. https://www.churchofengland.org/news-and-media/news-and-statements/church-and-legacy-slavery
18. Rom 8:17; Eph 2: 6; Rev 5:10

19. https://en.wikipedia.org/wiki/1_Timothy_2:12
20. https://www.biblestudytools.com/lexicons/hebrew/kjv/basar.html

Chapter 14: The Final Battle

1. Ps 139: 13; 1 Thess 2:12; Is 43:1-4; Is 44:2; Coll 1: 16; Jer 31:3
2. 1 John 5:4
3. Eph 1:5; John 1:12
4. Rom 8:17
5. Heb 9:11-15; 1 Peter 2:9
6. Is 43: 16-21
7. Rom 8: 28
8. Ps 68: 11
9. Eph 6:10-18
10. 1 Tim 6: 12
11. Prov 16: 3; 1 Cor 10:31
12. Heb 12: 1-3
13. Eph 4:1; 1 Thess 2:12
14. Ps 107: 2-3; Acts 4: 19-20
15. Eph 4:11-13; Deut 5: 5
16. Gen 2:18; 1 Cor 12:26
17. Matt 28: 16-20; Eph 2: 20-22; Eph 4: 11-13
18. Rev 12: 11; Luke 14: 33
19. Amos 9: 13-14
20. Prov 27: 17
21. Heb 12: 1-2
22. 1 John 4: 4
23. Rom 8: 19
24. Is 10:27; Is 52:2; Is 54; Micah 7:8
25. Is 60:1; Song of Songs 2: 10-13
26. 2 Cor 5:17; Is 42:9; Is 48:6; Luke 17: 32
27. Is 54
28. Heb 11: 1
29. Ps 27:13
30. Ps 107:2-3

Application Workbook

To make the most of this workbook I'd encourage you to complete the relevant sections below after you complete reading each chapter of the book.

> *Key Takeaway*: Write down any key ideas or text that stood out for you, or any a-ha! thoughts or burning questions you had, as you read this chapter.
>
> *Reflection:* A question or statement to encourage deeper reflection on the content of the chapter and what this means for you in your context.
>
> *Call to Action*: An encouragement to practically apply in your life any new learning or ideas you have gained as a result of reflecting on what you've read.

In this way you can keep your thoughts fresh, and track how your thoughts and ideas develop as you progress through the book. You may wish to use a separate journal to freely record all your responses, thoughts and accompanying prayers.

You may complete this workbook as a personal development exercise, or as a group discussion with close friends or bible study partners, as you explore the biblical scriptures and what this means for your calling and your walk with God.

Part 1: Women's God-Given Identity and Calling

Introduction: The Race and Calling

Key Takeaway:

Reflection:

How does the description of the race compare with your experiences as a Christian woman?

We are called first and foremost into an intimate relationship with God our Savior (Deut 6:4–5). How would you describe your current relationship with God?

By which names have you inadvertently been living which are in contrast to what God calls you and says you are?

Call to Action: What is the next small action you wish to commit to for the next week, as you start the journey of prayerfully considering and reflecting on your calling in God?

Chapter 1: In the Beginning

Key Takeaway:

Reflection:

How does this chapter's exploration of the Creation story and the dominion mandate given by God compare with what you have understood of these events (Genesis 1-2)?

What have you understood to be your mandate and calling as a Christian woman and how does this compare to the text in this chapter about the meaning of *ezer*?

What are your thoughts about the multi-generational call of women?

Call to Action: Complete below three '*I am*' statements you believe and want to embrace in your life about your eternal identity in God (you can reference relevant bible verses to support your statements).

I am ……

I am ……

I am ……

Chapter 2: The Fall

Key Takeaway:

Reflection:

What are your thoughts about the enmity that God places between the woman and Satan (Gen 3: 15)?

What are your thoughts about the fallen relationship between the man and woman explored in this chapter (Gen 3: 16)?

Call to Action: In the next year, how can you practically model in your life the value and role of women in God's Great Commission to other women and girls.

Chapter 3: A World out of Balance

Key Takeaway:

Reflection:

What are your thoughts about the historic place of women in societies across the world?

What have been your experiences as you've worked out your calling in the marketplace and in the church?

Call to Action: Based on the insight you've gained in this chapter, what would you like to address and take action on in your daily life, in the next year?

Part 2: Women's Calling Throughout the Scriptures

Chapter 4: The Role of Women in the Old Testament

Key Takeaway:

Reflection:

What are your thoughts about the stories of Old Testament women included in this chapter?

What, if anything, surprised you about these women's stories?

Having considered these women's stories, what do you believe you have learnt about God's approach to women in the mandate on earth?

Call to Action: List 1 - 3 characteristics or approaches demonstrated by any of the women included in this chapter which you would like to commit to prayerfully developing in your own life in the next year, to support your calling in God.

Chapter 5: Jesus and the Calling of Women

Key Takeaway:

Reflection:

What, if anything, in this chapter surprised you about Jesus' approach and interaction with women?

What do you think about the many firsts that Jesus afforded women, tasks which in that culture would've been seen as the spiritual privilege of men?

What are your thoughts about the role and actions of women in Jesus' ministry?

Call to Action: Having reflected on what this chapter illuminates about Jesus' views and approach, complete the following statement for yourself and as relevant to your life:

Jesus, thank you ....

Chapter 6: The Role of Women in the 1st Century Church

Key Takeaway:

Reflection:

What have you learnt in this chapter that you did not know or had not considered before?

What are your thoughts about Peter's declaration of Joel's prophecy at the birthing of the Christian church on the Day of Pentecost (Acts 2: 17-18)?

What are your thoughts and understanding about Paul's declaration in Galatians 3: 26-29?

Call to Action: Write down one action or intention that you've learnt about the 1st century church that you want to see practically implemented in your life in the next year.

Part 3: Case Study - The Calling of Mary

Chapter 7: A Woman Called

Key Takeaway:

Reflection:

What have you learnt in this chapter that you did not know or had not considered before?

How does this picture of the coming of Christ inform the understanding you've had up until now regarding the circumstances of Christ's birth?

Call to Action: Pray this next week that God would continue to grow your understanding and insight into God's redemptive work through the miraculous coming of Christ and his death and resurrection.

Chapter 8: Highly Favored

Key Takeaway:

Reflection:

What does this chapter reveal about the various ways God speaks to us about his will for our lives?

What are your thoughts about Elizabeth's role in Mary's life as Mary faces this unexpected calling?

Mary faced the possibility of walking out her calling as a single woman. What do you think are the challenges for single Christians in the church today as they walk out their calling?

Call to Action: Mary surrendered to God's calling. What do you need to surrender to God in order to come under his will and calling for your life? Pray to God about this for the next week.

Chapter 9: A Woman's Mandate

Key Takeaway:

Reflection:

What have you read in this chapter that you had not considered before?

Which details that you've read about Mary's calling up until this chapter particularly strike you?

How does Mary's status and background influence your view about the calling you have in Christ?

Call to Action: Write down any preconceived ideas you may realise you've personally held regarding what may be required of you to be called by God. In the next week, reflect and pray about how these may have influenced your walk in the calling God has for you.

Chapter 10: Partnership in Marriage

Key Takeaway:

Reflection:

What have you read in this chapter that surprised you or that you had not considered before?

What are your thoughts on Joseph's obedience to the call of God?

As a woman what in this chapter, if anything, do you find challenging with regards to your calling in God?

Call to Action: In the next week, pray for your own marriage (if you're married) and the marriages of your friends and family, that God would continue to strengthen, protect and grow these unions.

If you are single and wish to be married, pray in the next week that God would continue to grow you and your understanding of your role and calling as a woman in your future marriage.

Chapter 11: A Woman of Substance

Key Takeaway:

Reflection:

How has this exploration of Mary's character and actions during her lifetime challenged you in your walk of faith?

What are your thoughts on Jesus' words in Luke 11: 27-28?

What fears, doubts or beliefs hold you back from fully stepping out in faith and trusting God?

Call to Action: Write down one small step or action you will take in the next week to build your faith in God and his will for your life?

Part 4: The Call to Women and the Church today

Chapter 12: Women and their Calling in the Church

Key Takeaway:

Reflection:

What is your understanding of the place of spiritual gifts in the mission and function of the contemporary church?

What are your thoughts on 1 Tim 2: 11-12?

Call to Action: In the next week, pray to God for wisdom and insight about how he wants you to maturely use the spiritual gifts that he has given you, or that you desire to have, for the building up of the church.

Chapter 13: The Time is Now

Key Takeaway:

Reflection:

What are your thoughts on the role of the ecclesia to be salt and light in this generation?

What do you believe are the greatest challenges we the ecclesia face in effectively walking out our calling in the Great Commission, in this generation?

What do you think Paul meant in Galatians 3: 26-29 when he said ‘neither male nor female’?

Call to Action: Read the parable of the talents in Matt 25: 14-30. This next week, pray for God to reveal to you any talents, spiritual giftings or instructions from God that you have hidden or buried out of fear, doubt or an unwillingness to bear the cost of walking in that calling?

Chapter 14: The Final Battle

Key Takeaway:

Reflection:

What is your understanding or experience of the spiritual battle that faces us as children of God?

How does God's victory over Satan, sin and death affect your approach to how you live your life?

Reflect on the ways in which you can boldly and courageously embrace your identity and your calling in your life.

Call to Action: Write down your own personal battle cry for the spiritual battle of the ages in which you are engaged (you may choose to declare a bible verse as your battle cry). Once you've written it down, stand up you Warrior of God and say it out loud, with a roar and a shout of conviction! Shout it out as you can't stay silent because of what you know. Place the written battle cry in a place of prominence as a constant reminder and encouragement of who you are in Christ and what you are here for.

Commit to Active Prayer:

- Pray for yourself – for increased faith, boldness and courage to embrace your full and true identity in Christ, and for clarity on your mandate and calling in him.
- Pray for your marriage – that it may reflect the marital relationship God intended when he created the first husband and wife with a shared purpose and destiny.
- Pray for your family – that what you model in the home and with each other may reflect God's higher intention for his ecclesia.
- Pray for your church – that it may fix its eyes on Jesus and submit to his Holy Spirit working in and through the lives of all the members of its Body. That all believers may be liberated, equipped and empowered for the work of the advancement of the kingdom of God.
- Pray for the global ecclesia – That it may grow in strength, boldness and deep faith and take up its mantle as a called out, set apart people who are willing to be counter cultural in order to make God known and to bring righteous transformation to communities around the globe.

Explore Your Unique Calling

We are to remember that our primary calling is unto God, our Lord and Savior, and that we are called to love him with all our heart, soul, mind and strength (Matthew 22: 36-37). We are also called to love others and share the gospel with all people. So before you start to explore your unique calling, take time first to examine and reflect on where you are in your relationship with God, your repentance of your sin, and in the full surrender of your life to his will and purpose. The bible tells us we are saved by faith and salvation in Christ alone.

We are called to a life of faith that is not about desiring an almighty God to fulfil the plans and vision we have for our lives, but rather we are to be obedient to God's will and serve God in his plan and vision for our lives, whatever that may require of us. It is only out of this posture and foundation of full devotion, intimate relationship and surrender that we can fully learn to hear and accurately discern God's unique calling for our lives. Jesus tells us that his followers know his voice (John 10:27-28).

In exploring your unique calling, consider the clues that God leaves you. Complete the following sections on the following page.

What desires have been stirring in your heart?	
What past words of instruction from God have you received? (Have these been tested?)	
What spiritual gifts have you seen the evidence of in your life?	
What are you passionate about (What makes you come alive? When are you in 'your zone'?)	
What keeps you up at night (what in life / society gets you fired up or angry)?	
Which societal needs stir you?	
What do you excel at?	
What are your strengths?	
What do others tell you your strengths and talents are (what are you frequently complimented on or thanked for)?	
Where have you seen proof of positive impact and God's anointing on your efforts?	
What sectors of society / spheres of influence are you active in?	
What opportunities to serve are available to you?	

Reflection: Once you have completed these above, reflect on the areas of overlap and what that may be telling you about your unique calling. Write this down.

Call to Action: Commit this to God in prayer and ask him to reveal to you his will and unique calling for your life. Put your fears and doubts in God's hands.

Pray for courage and boldness to surrender to God's will and take the next steps into your calling. Consider what you may need to sacrifice in order to do this.

Engage with a coach, mentor, counsellor and/or trusted friend to support you and hold you accountable in your journey of discerning and taking appropriate action as you walk out your calling.

Acknowledgements

About the Author

Renay Taylor is an experienced executive coach, mentor and leadership trainer. She has over 25 years' international leadership experience in the healthcare and education sectors. Since 2005 she's used her bespoke coaching and training solutions to empower her global clients to level up, make an impact, and operate at their full potential in a way that is true to their values and beliefs and who they are.

She is a member of the John Maxwell Team of international leadership speakers, trainers and coaches. She is a certified DISC Behavioral Consultant, holds a Diploma in Transformational Coaching, and is accredited by the International Coaching Federation.

She has been a committed Christian for over 30 years. She has led and taught both in her professional roles and in the Christian church. She is particularly passionate about equipping women to step into their God-given purpose and calling. The Call of a Woman is her first book.

www.renaytaylor.com

contact@renaytaylor.com

Printed in Poland
by Amazon Fulfillment
Poland Sp. z o.o., Wrocław

31959771R00094